What people are saying about

Jesus Ev...

"Wendy is not only a sister in ministry but a sweet friend who shares my passion for helping women learn that putting our trust in Jesus and truly believing He has our present and futures in His hands is the only way to endure all the uncertainties and struggles of life and maintain peace in our hearts along the way. *Jesus Everlasting* not only helps readers grasp the gift Jesus really is, but also the importance of making God's Word a priority in our lives and the immense blessings we receive when we do so."

Tracie Miles, bestselling author of five books and
director of COMPEL Training at Proverbs 31 Ministries

"Every day we're faced with the battles, baggage, bumps, and bruises of this world. And every day we look for answers amidst the noise to find clarity, direction, hope, and peace. Wendy's latest book, *Jesus Everlasting*, encapsulates the brilliant solution we're all looking for. Each page points to a beautiful new discovery that will help you navigate life's biggest struggles, while giving you joy and assurance in the process. It's a must-read!"

Leah DiPascal, cohost of *Lighten Up Sweet Pea
Podcast,* former contributing writer to Proverbs 31
Ministries: Encouragement Today and First5 App

"Wendy's book *Jesus Everlasting* made my soul sing! With authenticity and biblical depth, Wendy reveals each loving layer of the Lord's attributes and character. What a blessed assurance to know we can lean on Jesus and He can bear the weight. After reading this book, I am confident you will be joining the choir to sing praises to the Lord who is worthy of worship, poised to be present, and ready for relationship. Lean in and sing on as you continue to discover the forever faithfulness of our Jesus Everlasting."

Rachael Adams, host of *The Love Offering Podcast*

"'Who do you say I am?' That's a question Jesus asked of His disciples, the men who walked with Him daily. It's also a question He asks of us today. I'm captivated with Wendy's warm and inviting way of introducing us to this same Jesus. When a sea of 'experts' overwhelm us with worldly advice, Wendy offers Jesus, the wise Counselor who truly listens and cares. When we feel alone and overwhelmed—and we all do—Wendy draws us in to meet Jesus our Defender, teaching us how to stand firm while battles rage in the heavenlies. Sprinkled with personal stories, this book helps us understand Jesus as Father and Friend. Each precious chapter reveals a powerful characteristic of the Son of God, and after each one, I imagine Wendy stepping back with a smile to allow the reader to spend time with Jesus through worship and journaling. Trust me, we need Jesus right now. In this book, Wendy reaches out, takes you by the hand, and leads you right to the very heart of our Savior. When you do, you'll be comforted, defended, cherished, and at peace."

Kelly Langston, author of five books, including
When God Gives a Dream and *40 Prayers for Perilous Times*

"In *Jesus Everlasting*, Wendy Pope invites readers to savor the Savior, so that we can celebrate the gift of Christ year-round. In each chapter, Wendy equips her readers to find relief for a troubled heart by rediscovering and contemplating the sweet benefits of Christ with childlike awe and wonder."

Titania Paige, author of *Come Home: A Redemptive Roadmap from Lust Back to Christ*

"In *Jesus Everlasting*, Wendy takes us on a deep journey of building our faith in the One who was given to us and who gave His life for us. Each chapter is rich with God's Word where we learn of the Lord's character, care, compassion, and conviction. The truths of Scripture Wendy shares grow and renew our relationship with the Lord. The love of our Savior is poured out on each page, and we are invited to drink deeply from the well of Living Water. Wendy writes with an eternal perspective, keeping our eyes on and highlighting the trustworthiness of our Counselor, Defender, Father, and Friend. Her best writing yet, Wendy reignited the zeal and fervor in my walk with the Lord."

Sharon Sloan, author of *SerenDIPity: Celebrating Dips, Faith & Friendship* (serendipitydipsbook.com), director of Women's Ministry at Grace Point (Newtown, PA)

From everlasting
to everlasting —
Jesus!

♡ Wendy
Is. 9:6

Jesus
Everlasting

Jesus Everlasting

Leaning on Our Counselor, Defender, Father, & Friend

Wendy Pope

DAVID C COOK

transforming lives together

JESUS EVERLASTING
Published by David C Cook
4050 Lee Vance Drive
Colorado Springs, CO 80918 U.S.A.

Integrity Music Limited, a Division of David C Cook
Brighton, East Sussex BN1 2RE, England

The graphic circle C logo is a registered trademark of David C Cook.

Bible credits are listed in the back of the book.

Library of Congress Control Number 2021932775
ISBN 978-1-4347-1240-0
eISBN 978-0-8307-8128-7

© 2021 Wendy Pope

The Team: Susan McPherson, Laura Derico, Megan Stengel,
Jon Middel, Jack Campbell, Susan Murdock
Cover Design: James Hershberger
Cover Photo: Getty Images

Printed in the United States of America
First Edition 2021

1 2 3 4 5 6 7 8 9 10

061621

To My Grover Girls
Bronwyn, Christie, Leslie, and Sharon.
Jesus brought us together. Jesus holds us together.
And because of Jesus we will be together forever.

Contents

Acknowledgments

Malcom and Judy, thank you for the amazing views and safe place to pen all four of my manuscripts. OIB and your place is my home-away-from-home.

My amazing David C Cook publishing team, wow—this is our sixth project together. I don't feel like I know any more about publishing now than I did before *Wait and See*. You guys just drag me over the finish line every time. Thank you for your patience. I write the book, Laura massages the words, and Jack makes sure those words obey all the rules. Annette and Susan work hard to get the message out in creative ways. Thank you so much for all that you do for me, and all the authors who are blessed to partner with DCC.

Thank you to my Proverbs 31 Ministries family. I served the Lord with you for almost two decades, and you afforded me ministry opportunities I wouldn't have had otherwise. Thank you for your investment in me.

Blythe, thank you for love, encouragement, friendship, and guidance through the crazy publishing process. You've been on my side from the start, believing in me and the messages trusted to my care, even when I didn't. I look forward to the publishing future with you. Love you and your precious family so much.

Daddy and Momma, as I write this book, you've been married sixty-six years. Daddy, we just celebrated your ninetieth birthday. Mom, we will soon gather to celebrate your eighty-seventh birthday. I thank the Lord for your long lives and endearing love story. You've loved me and Wes so well.

Scott, Blaire, and Griffin, besides my relationship with the Lord, the three of you are the best part of my life. The cry of my heart is to live a life that leaves a legacy of loving the Lord and His Word above all else. If I fail to do this, then I've failed in my calling. Chase the Lord, live His Word, and the life you've always longed for is the life you will live.

Foreword

"In the beginning was the Word, and the Word was with God, and the Word was God. He was with God in the beginning…. The Word became flesh and made his dwelling among us" (John 1:1–2, 14 NIV).

That "Word [who] became flesh" is the One of whom Isaiah the prophet foretold hundreds of years before it came to pass: "For to us a child is born, to us a son is given, and the government will be on his shoulders. And he will be called Wonderful Counselor, Mighty God, Everlasting Father, Prince of Peace" (Isa. 9:6 NIV). That's our Jesus.

Who is Jesus to you? Do you believe that you can be satisfied—truly satisfied—by Him? Can you agree with the words to the hymn that boasts, "All that thrills my soul is Jesus"?

About twenty years ago I found myself pondering these very questions as I walked through *Living Free* by Beth Moore. The powerful teachings in this Bible study were life-altering for me. In the book, the reader is encouraged to "explore five benefits God supplies us by His grace." As I came upon week 4, the benefit for the week was titled "To Find Satisfaction in God." I'm about to make a difficult confession here: that heading led me into full-on questioning God. I can remember saying, "Really, God? How can I find my satisfaction in You? You're invisible, for heaven's sake. You're not a tangible body that can hug me, console me, carry on an audible conversation with me. I'm so thankful for You, for Jesus, and Your Holy Spirit. I'm thankful for the many blessings You've provided. I know that all things come from Your hand. But can You really satisfy all of my longings?"

I'll never forget what happened immediately after that. I went to refill my coffee cup. As I poured that morning nectar, I heard two words: *Everlasting Portion.* Those words—not audible, just in my heart and mind—not naturally being my normal thought process, caused me to ask, "God, was that You?"

I settled back into my chair. My conversation continued. "Lord, I don't understand. What does that mean?"

Silence.

I prayed, "Lord, I know that was You. Help me to get what You're saying to me."

More silence.

I carried on that seemingly one-sided conversation with, "Okay, Lord, I know that You are the everlasting God. You existed before time began and will be forever. I realize that as believers we will spend eternity with You in heaven. That communion will be everlasting. I think I grasp the concept of 'everlasting.' But what does 'portion' have to do with it?"

I listened again, but nothing.

I continued to ramble. "I'm at a loss here. When I think of 'portion,' all I can think of is in reference to the food on our plates. If we're eating properly, our plates contain the appropriate amounts of foods that provide the nutrition necessary to keep us healthy."

I think I heard the Wonderful Counselor say, "Go with that."

"All right, so there's not too much on the plate. Not too little. The proper amount for that particular meal. Not enough for the whole day. Not enough for tomorrow. Just what we need."

And I got the message. HE is our everlasting portion. Always just what we need. For the day. For the hour. For the moment. Yet always at the ready for what we need next.

What do you need, my friend? What is your heart longing for today? Are you searching for satisfaction? Is there an emptiness that cries out to be filled?

Do you look at other godly women and think that along with them you want to be able to say, "All that thrills my soul is Jesus"?

God's Word holds within it the answers to our deepest longings, to our every need.

Are you seeking satisfaction there? Jeremiah 29:12–13 tells us, "Then you will call on me and come and pray to me, and I will listen to you. You will seek me and find me when you seek me with all your heart" (NIV).

Are you longing for comfort? In 2 Corinthians 1:3–4, Paul proclaimed, "Praise be to the God and Father of our Lord Jesus Christ, the Father of compassion and the God of all comfort, who comforts us in all our troubles, so that we can comfort those in any trouble with the comfort we ourselves receive from God" (NIV).

Do you need strength? Isaiah 40:28–29 reminds us of the ultimate source: "Do you not know? Have you not heard? The LORD is the everlasting God, the Creator of the ends of the earth. He will not grow tired or weary, and his understanding no one can fathom. He gives strength to the weary and increases the power of the weak" (NIV).

Do you need forgiveness? In Psalm 51:1–2, David prayed (and we can do so in his words), "Have mercy on me, O God, according to your unfailing love; according to your great compassion blot out my transgressions. Wash away all my iniquity and cleanse me from my sin" (NIV). And 1 John 1:9 says, "If we confess our sins, he is faithful and just and will forgive us our sins and purify us from all unrighteousness" (NIV).

Is peace seemingly beyond your grasp? Philippians 4:6–7 encourages us, "Do not be anxious about anything, but in every situation, by prayer and petition, with thanksgiving, present your requests to God. And the peace of God, which transcends all understanding, will guard your hearts and your minds in Christ Jesus" (NIV).

Is love what you crave? Have you been "looking for love in all the wrong places"? There is a God-sized void in each of us that only He can fill—with His love. In Jeremiah 31:3, the Lord is quoted as saying, "I have loved you with an everlasting love; I have drawn you with unfailing kindness" (NIV).

Jesus is the answer to our every need.

God's Word is truth from beginning to end. He authored the chronicles of creation, focusing on the pinnacle of His creation: man and woman. Even before His design was complete, He knew this man, this woman, and every human being to follow would need a Savior—but He already had a plan in the works. Through the act of Jesus becoming flesh and ultimately giving His life as a sacrifice for us, God orchestrated the ultimate culmination of His narrative through the gift of the Holy Spirit. The Spirit draws us to the Word and helps us understand all that lies within—and all that He provides for us.

I can't think of anyone I know who loves the Word of God more, who digs deeper in study, who believes every single truth and promise found within more than my sister-of-the-heart, Wendy Pope. She has set up the banqueting table so beautifully, and the feast is ready! I believe that this book will feed your soul, as Wendy guides you toward understanding the many facets of our Everlasting Jesus.

Kristi M. Butler

Introduction

I don't know anyone who doesn't like to receive a gift, especially an unexpected gift. Oh, we like to appear humble and offer a polite "Oh, you shouldn't have," while down deep inside we are screaming like a five-year-old who got her first American Girl doll or a long-awaited Easy-Bake Oven. We open the gift with great care so as not to tear the wrapping—untying the neatly tied bow, using our fingernails to pull the paper from the creased corners closed by two-sided tape. Shrills of delight fill the air as we reveal the surprise in our hands.

And what about those *expected* gifts for Christmas, birthdays, and anniversaries? (Unless you are one of those unfortunate souls who has a birthday *and* anniversary near Christmas, then you get the all-in-one-gift: Happy Annibirthmas!) We know the gift is coming. Perhaps we've dropped hints to our loved one, or our loved one has disclosed a few clues. In any case, there's some special occasion, and a gift is rightly expected. We don't have to hide our enthusiasm in opening the gift. We give no regard to decorum; ribbons and wrapping paper take flight as we tear into our *expected* package.

What happens, however, when the gift *isn't* what we'd wanted? What is our response when the gift we were expecting isn't at all what we expected?

We're going to hang out together for a while and examine a gift that was expected but, when it came, wasn't exactly as expected.

> ✝ *What is our response when the*
> *gift we were expecting isn't*
> *at all what we expected?*

Isaiah was a prophet who lived during the time when the nation of Israel was seized by the Assyrians, something God providentially permitted because of the nation's habitual sins of disobedience and idolatry. Isaiah prophesied many things about the future of the nation during the Judean kingships of Uzziah, Jotham, Ahaz, and Hezekiah. But perhaps his greatest words of prophecy surrounded the promise of a Messiah—a man who would come, rule, and reign. The people of Israel thought they would finally receive justice through this Messiah. Maybe you've read this promise of hope in Isaiah 9:6:

> For a child is born to us,
>   a son is given to us.
> The government will rest on his shoulders.
>   And he will be called:
> Wonderful Counselor, Mighty God,
>   Everlasting Father, Prince of Peace.

The expected gift was the Messiah. The unexpected part was a baby.

The nation of Israel was looking for—expecting—a *man* who would lead and save them. Maybe a warrior or a wise governor, but definitely a full-grown person. Finally the people of Israel would be recognized as the people of Yahweh (the Hebrew term for "God"). They would be esteemed on the worldwide stage as a nation of power and authority.

But what came instead? A baby, named Jesus, born to a teenager and a carpenter, seven hundred years after the prophecy was foretold. A gift expected, but not as expected.

> ✝ *The expected gift was the Messiah. The unexpected part was a baby.*

Oh, the places we will go together, both expected and unexpected, as we unwrap this gift! I hope you have your Bible, a highlighter, and a pen close by. We have provided Bible study material as well as pages for you to journal all that God is teaching you. You can expect to hear from God through the whispers of the Holy Spirit. Wouldn't it be so fun if we could sit in the same room and do Bible study together in a big circle? I can't be with you, but I hope you will grab a friend, or a group of friends, to read and study together.

Before we move to chapter 1, let me address the elephant in the room—no, this is not a Christmas book. Yes, we are going to talk about the birth of Jesus. But Jesus is more than a reason to celebrate for one season. He is more than a figure in a nativity scene. Certainly, many Christians joyfully celebrate the birth of Jesus, and in his prophecy, Isaiah referred to this child as a gift, "a son is given to us." But do you ever wonder why we don't make more of this gift every day of the year, as much as we do at Christmastime (or maybe also at Easter)?

Do you ever wonder why we aren't struck by God's wise plans any given Wednesday, when our schedules for the week are already scattered? Or why we don't feel like singing songs about joy coming to the world when we are in the middle of reading the morning headlines? Why do we doubt God's faithfulness when our bank accounts look empty (maybe in the cold light of January, when those Christmas bills come due)? And why is it so easy to feel peaceful at a candlelit Christmas Eve service but so hard to find peace in the middle of a summertime traffic jam, when we're late for a meeting and the A/C decides this is the day to die? In other words, why can't it feel more like Christmas every day?

I've already given you a hint to the answer—it was just hidden in another question. Remember how I asked, "What is our response when the gift we were expecting isn't at all what we expected?" Maybe the reason we have a hard time feeling like it's Christmas every day is because we have wrong expectations of what Christmas really means. And maybe we have ripped that paper off the gift of Jesus so quickly that we've forgotten to take time to understand and enjoy and experience the transforming power of the Messiah.

In our time together, we are going to unwrap this gift slowly, not ripping the paper or tearing the bow, but chapter by chapter we will discover the wonder of Jesus and His place in our lives every day. He is the gift that goes on, often in surprising ways. Jesus is our:

- Wonderful Counselor, who knows us better than anyone;
- Mighty God, who stands with us and for us;
- Everlasting Father, who calls to us and comes back for us;
- Prince of Peace, who stops and steadies us.

In our study, we'll meet five women who had one-on-one, transformational encounters with Jesus. They met Him as their Counselor, Defender, Father, and yes, even as a Friend. They leaned on the certainty of His wisdom, power, faithfulness, and peace when trouble and stress surrounded them. They found out firsthand why He was born to be celebrated every day. And so can we.

Are you ready to start unwrapping? Me too! I'll meet you in chapter 1!

Everlasting Thoughts

I know what you're thinking. *My thoughts don't even last a minute—much less for "ever."* If you're like me, you walk in a room and forget why you're there and what you were looking for, plus you remember five other things you forgot to do in the last room you were in. That's what is so great about this book! At the end of each chapter, you can record your thoughts right here, right now. Just jot them down as soon as they pop in your head, and then later you can come back and sort out all your relevant revelations and insightful inspirations. Don't erase, edit, or omit. Just put pen or pencil to paper and listen to what God is trying to teach you through His Word.

What was one of the best *expected* gifts you ever received (something given to you on a holiday or other occasion when a gift is customary)? What made it special?

What was an unexpected gift you received? What was surprising about it?

Whether you've spent lots of time with Jesus or are just getting introduced to Him, take a minute and list some of your impressions about who Jesus is:

One of the Old Testament prophecies that points to Jesus is in Isaiah 53:2:

> My servant grew up in the LORD's presence like a
>   tender green shoot,
>   like a root in dry ground.
> There was nothing beautiful or majestic about his
>   appearance,
>   nothing to attract us to him.

This verse states that there was nothing about Jesus's physical appearance to attract people to Him. But what do you think attracts people to Jesus now? What attracts you?

Challenge: Read all of Isaiah 53 this week and highlight or note the verses that point to Jesus.

Leaning on the Music

I LOVE a church choir! It doesn't matter if people are dressed in their casual Sunday best swaying to the beat of the latest contemporary Christian release or standing stoically in choir robes gripping a black music folder singing an ancient hymn; there's just something about a choir that generates the power of praise. My parents not only instilled this love in me but also nurtured it with their commitment to our church choir. While most Wednesday nights during rehearsal I was running around the church campus or sliding under the pews, I somehow fell head over heels in love with church music. You'll hear more about my love for the choir in chapter 1, but for now, let's talk about music.

Music has the power to stir a soul to weep, laugh, or shout, and a body to bounce, dance, or slide. Your heart can travel to a time long ago or to a place you've always wanted to visit. Now add the word *worship* in front of the word *music* and that power becomes holy. Choral pieces, orchestral pieces, the quick upbeat rhythm of the latest Big Daddy Weave single, or the liturgical flow of "How Great Thou Art" are all designed to direct us to the One worthy of our worship, the Lord Jesus Christ.

I was raised on hymns. It thrills my soul that I can sing every word of "A Mighty Fortress Is Our God" and "Be Thou My Vision."

Equally filling my soul are new songs like "There Was Jesus" and "Ain't No Grave." Music is a part of my being. It connects me to the Father in an intimate way. Do you feel the same? Maybe you're singing your favorite song of worship right now. I'd love to know what it is.

After each chapter, I'm going to give you a glimpse into the music of my life, the music that helps lead me to Jesus Everlasting, and the music I lean on to remind me of His presence every day. You'll hear about some of my favorite songs and why they are special to me. I won't ask you to sing, but I can almost guarantee that you will. Wouldn't it be fun if we put together an online meeting and just sang for a while? The music would carry the cares of our hearts and the snares of the world out of our reach. We will sing together one day, only it won't be online—it will be in the throne room of our God. Oh, I can't wait! Will you meet me there? I'll be sitting with the second sopranos.

Chapter 1

A Son Who Was Given to Us

Everyone gets excited about the arrival of a new baby. There was a time when social media blew up with the "heading to the hospital" pics followed by the "at the hospital" pics, then "the baby is here" pics. The most recent craze is the "gender-reveal party." The mommy- and daddy-to-be invite close family and friends to a small gathering where they reveal the gender of their little bundle of joy in some very unusual way.

For example, the future dad hits a golf ball that explodes on contact, spraying pink dust all over the yard—"It's a girl!" Or the mommy-to-be approaches a bouquet of balloons with a sharp pin. She pops each balloon until one blasts blue glitter—"It's a boy!" These reveals are videoed and posted all over social media. The world knows that, within a few months, a baby is coming and what kind of clothes to buy said baby. So much hype! We've come so far. Just think—back in the day when my babies were born, we sent announcements in an envelope via snail mail, a.k.a. the postal service.

Jesus had a reveal announcement long before it was a thing. He's always ahead of the curve. Without any fanfare or pics to prove it happened, Isaiah heralded to the world that a boy was coming. The timing of this hot-off-the-press declaration was very interesting. The coming child would arrive … not in five months, or even five years. This child would arrive more than seven hundred years in the future. How's *that* for advance notice?

At That Time

When studying Scripture, it's important to gain a broad understanding of the context, such as what was happening and who wrote or spoke at the time the words were written. It's very dangerous and, might I say, disrespectful to the authority of Scripture to cherry-pick what verses we want to claim as support for our statements. And so, without becoming too deep and possibly overwhelmed with Old Testament history, let's try to get a general view of what was happening at the time Isaiah proclaimed the birth announcement of Jesus. And you know what? Maybe it's a good idea to learn a little bit more about Isaiah too—the man behind the prophecy.

Isaiah's name means "Yahweh (God) is salvation," which is completely understandable, since he was a prophet of God. He lived in Judah, in the southern kingdom of Israel. The nation of Israel—the people set apart by God to be His very own special people—had divided into two. The northern kingdom was made up of ten unruly tribes governed by even more unruly kings, men who wanted their own way rather than seeking God's. The southern kingdom was made up of the other two tribes of Jacob.

Isaiah heard the call of God in a vision (Isa. 6). Even though Isaiah lived in the south, his assignment was to issue warnings to the north.

He was to face these tribes who had turned away from God and tell them of the impending invasion of the Assyrians and how they would conquer Israel. Quite an assignment, right? I think I'd rather sign up to be on the "Bathroom Check Team" or to colead the middle school boys' choir than to be the one to speak of God's judgment to a disobedient group of people. Nonetheless, Isaiah embraced his assignment and is one of the most well known of all the Old Testament prophets.

✝ *God is a redeemer of all things lost, thrown away, and forgotten.*

Despite Isaiah's warnings, the ten tribes eventually reaped the consequences of their sin and were completely conquered by the Assyrians, an enemy nation. These ten tribes were never heard of again after the invasion, but the land, the land was always God's. And God is a redeemer of all things lost, thrown away, and forgotten. He is a God of love, grace, mercy, and justice. Isaiah 9:6 (which we will study more in a bit) is God's promise of redemption and hope and the fulfillment of a covenant for His people and His land.

Before That Time

Before pandemonium filled the dusty streets, before pride and idolatry ran rampant in Israel, there was a good king. Not a *sinless* king, but a good king … a king God called "a man after my own heart" (Acts 13:22). David was Israel's greatest king. He was the man God chose to be king of His people. God loved David so much that He entered into a covenant, or agreement, with him and with the people of Israel.

This was an unconditional contract, meaning God would fulfill His part of the agreement without restrictions or requirements of David. This covenant became well known among God's people, and they longed for it to be fulfilled. From one generation to the next, through national divisions, and from king to king, God's people fully expected Him to come through on His promises, which were mainly regarding these three topics:

- a promised land, safe and secure, for the nation of Israel (2 Sam. 7:10);
- the fact that the Messiah—a chosen king—would come from the line of David (vv. 11–12); and
- that this newly established kingdom would last forever (v. 13).

This covenant wasn't like the Mosaic Covenant (named after Moses), which required obedience in exchange for God's provision and protection. With this new covenant, God's people only had to anticipate that God's faithfulness would one day be realized. No conditions, just eager expectation, like what we have for the gifts we expect on our special occasions.

✝ *From one generation to the next,*
God's people fully expected Him to
come through on His promises.

So you see now, this is how Jesus's birth would fulfill the Davidic Covenant. For generations, as the people suffered under unjust leaders and the oppression of their enemies, this promise of good news was looked for and longed for. *Finally there will come a day,* they thought, *when evil will no longer win, and oppression will cease.* Unfortunately, the people who heard this herald would not see its realization, and neither would their children or their grandchildren. Yet each generation knew of the Davidic Covenant and talked about it and expected to see it fulfilled.

The Promise for All Time

With some history in our hip pocket, let's spend some time understanding the prophetic promise; then we will tie it all up with a beautiful bow and connect the gift to you and me. Let's review the prophecy in Isaiah 9:6:

> For a child is born to us,
> a son is given to us.

The government will rest on his shoulders.
And he will be called:
Wonderful Counselor, Mighty God,
Everlasting Father, Prince of Peace.

Recall what we said earlier about the north part of Israel—how the Assyrians, a neighboring nation, conquered the ten tribes of this region, which was also known as Samaria. The territory was completely overtaken and the people became known as the lost tribes. What the Israelites could not know then was that this was just the beginning of centuries of being defeated and conquered and occupied. But still, even for those alive at the time, this was obviously a huge moment in the story of Israel, and it was noted by the people of the south and put into historical accounts to be remembered for the generations to come.

And of course, God saw this moment too.

Nothing on earth is unseen by God—nothing. He saw the sins of the world and instructed Noah to spare the only righteous people on earth, Noah's own family (Gen. 6:5–22). God saw Hagar when she ran from the unfortunate situation of bearing Abraham's child while he was married to Sarah (Gen. 16). He saw Joseph in prison before this mistreated son of Jacob was made prime minister of Egypt and saved his family from the famine (Gen. 39:19–23). God saw His people enslaved in Egypt and appointed Moses as their deliverer (Ex. 3:7–12). He saw Jonah in the belly of a big fish (Jon. 1:17), and He saw David's sins of adultery and murder (2 Sam. 12:7–10).

✝ Nothing on earth is unseen by God—nothing.

God sees. He is *El Roi*, the "God who sees." He knew exactly what was happening in Israel. Just as He took action in every situation described above, God acted on behalf of the disobedient and disappointing Israelites. He sent a word of hope through Isaiah.

One day all of this will be over. Order will be restored. Justice will be served. Evil will no longer rule. I'm going to send someone to take care of all this and more. This person will come as a child, and He will be wonderful from the moment He is conceived. He will grow in wisdom and will be the wisest of all kings, offering counsel to all who need it. This Wonderful One will be mighty in His defense of you. No longer will you fear a hostile takeover from neighboring nations or individuals set out to perpetrate evil on you. His rule will never end. His kingdom will be everlasting. You will be able to trust His authority and leadership forever. And peace ... oh, there will be peace, because His very nature generates it. Peace and justice will hold hands under His leadership, and those living under His rule will dance to the harmony of the song of freedom that His leadership will compose.

Well, that's how I paraphrase it.

Oh, can you even imagine the hope Isaiah's prophecy sparked as it echoed through the war-torn hearts of God's people? Spoken directly to the people who had heard and seen what was happening to northern Israel, this prophecy must have brought tranquility to their trepid souls, especially since Egypt was rising as a superpower and threatening a takeover too. God saw! He still loved them! He was sending someone, once again, to rescue them! So now they would be expecting rescue. They would expect a Wonderful Counselor, a Mighty God, an Everlasting Father, and a Prince of Peace. They would expect the One who would:

- offer shrewd counsel,
- fight their enemies for them,
- never leave them, and
- bring peace by overcoming their rivals.

But did they get the rescuer they were expecting? That's the question we'll find answers to as we view their expectations through the eyes of those who actually looked into the face of Jesus.

As we dive deeper into this verse, we have to keep in mind all the context we just inhaled. Isaiah couldn't have known at the time that the messages he was speaking might be read thousands of years later by people like us. And he did not know that around seven hundred years after he was delivering prophecies, the gift of the Son who was promised would become reality. As far as he knew, his audience was the people of God in Jerusalem and Judah. What was to be their eventual hope would become the eternal hope for everyone who believed in Jesus.

His Position

One of my highest aspirations as a young girl was to join the adult choir in my church. I remember the swelling of my insides when I finally reached eighteen and was assigned my choir robe cubby and black music folder. My parents had always been in the choir, so I was forced to sit in the sanctuary each Wednesday night for an hour and listen to rehearsal. To say I *sat* would not be totally honest; sometimes I slid under the pews or made those little triangle footballs out of paper and flicked them over the pews with the other kids of choir members. Anyway, I stayed, I heard, and I fell in love.

Something happened when the choir walked stately through those side doors into the choir loft. And those cantatas, for Easter and Christmas, they were something to behold! At the close of every Easter musical, the choir would sing one of the most difficult choral arrangements ever written—well, in my opinion. As I listened, I wondered how I would ever learn the song. The tempo was fast and the parts—oh!—the four parts were angelic but very challenging. How would I ever learn Handel's "Hallelujah" chorus and sing the hallelujahs at the right time? Whether or not you are familiar with the piece, I highly recommend you conduct an immediate online search for it and listen. It will take your breath away. With each octave change, the repetition of the Isaiah scripture heralding the rule and reign of the Messiah will make the hair on your arms stand up, and most likely will make you stand up and sing "Hallelujah" too.

Handel's Messiah was written by George Frideric Handel in 1741. Handel, with the scripture compilation by Charles Jennens, composed one of history's most notable pieces of music. While composing, he would refuse to eat and sleep, and often his servants would find him crying. Upon completion of the "Hallelujah" chorus, he told his assistant, "I did think I did see all Heaven before me, and the great God Himself seated on His throne, with His company of Angels."[1]

While the chorus doesn't lyrically point to the entire prophecy of Isaiah 9:6, we can draw a straight line to connect the prophetic words of the first part of the verse to its ultimate fulfillment penned by John in the book of Revelation (as taken from the King James Version):

- "Alleluia: for the Lord God omnipotent reigneth" (Rev. 19:6).
- "And he hath on his vesture and on his thigh a name written, KING OF KINGS, AND LORD OF LORDS" (v. 16).
- "The kingdoms of this world are become the kingdoms of our Lord, and of his Christ; and he shall reign for ever and ever" (11:15).

The first part of Isaiah 9:6 talks about a time when this king to come will have the responsibility of governing the people. Governing means not just dictating laws to people but also taking care of people and making sure they have what they need to be safe and secure. When Jesus first came to earth, He established the kingdom of God—a state of being in which people would live according to God's will, with justice and peace. This was not a kingdom that would fade away once Jesus left the earth, however. It was not a kingdom that would be taken over by the next king to come. Instead, as verse 7 goes on to say, this kingdom "will never end"; His kingdom of peace and justice and righteousness will continue on forever. Though not everyone recognizes Jesus's position as king now, a time will come when Jesus will come again and everyone will submit to His lordship.

His government and its peace
    will never end.
He will rule with fairness and justice from the
        throne of his ancestor David
    for all eternity.
The passionate commitment of the LORD of
        Heaven's Armies
    will make this happen! (9:7)

For the most part (and more so in Israel), the type of governing that Israel and Judah had known was oppressive, greedy, and
power-hungry, far from God-fearing and God-honoring. Therefore,
to hear about this new kingdom would have been music to their
ears—ushering in a "Hallelujah" chorus of relief to their souls.

His Person

The birth announcement in Isaiah not only established Jesus's position, it also described His personhood. Who wouldn't welcome and
be elated about the impending arrival of a Wonderful Counselor,
Mighty God, Everlasting Father, and Prince of Peace? No wonder the
people were looking for Him. They were hoping to meet someone
extraordinary.

Oh, it is so fun to study these attributes of our Savior! If you
are new to my writing, you don't know that I am a word-nerd and
most definitely a God's Word–nerd. Words fascinate me. One of my
favorite websites, no lie, is Dictionary.com. And the thesaurus makes
me want to jump out of my chair! And do you want to know what is

so incredibly funny about that? I'm a terrible speller. (I praise God for amazing editors, as well as the blue and red squiggly lines in my word-processing program that tell me when something is not exactly right.)

The Word—God's Word—captivates me. Some of my most exciting days are when I dig into Bible study. I investigate the meaning of a word, clicking on one link after another in online Bible study sites to find out the original Hebrew or Greek definitions and learn how different the meaning is compared to our modern English ideas. I could fill pages and pages with what I love about words, but truly my heart longs for you to love *the Word*. That is why I geek out on words in my books—I want you to see how thrilling it is to study the Bible, even when you aren't a Bible scholar.

As we're introduced to the Messiah, the attributes or titles given to Him in Isaiah 9:6 help us understand important aspects of His character. We'll investigate these further in each chapter and find out how Jesus connected in different ways with the people He encountered. My hope is that, by the end of this book, you will know Jesus more closely, and you'll see how these descriptions relate to anyone who calls on Him as their Savior. Let's get to know Him right now.

Wonderful Counselor, with or without the Comma

I know the title of this section might be causing a bend in your brow. But if you've ever heard *Handel's Messiah*, then you've heard the choir insert a huge pause between "Wonderful" and "Counselor." That's because in the King James Version, from which the text of the song was derived, the comma was there. But in later translations, the comma sometimes isn't there.

Apparently, there are at least a couple of different ways to understand the Hebrew in this section. The word we read now as "wonderful" was a noun in the Hebrew—*wonder*. Some translators have come to the conclusion that "Wonder" or "Wonderful" was one of the names of the child in the prophecy, rather than "Wonderful Counselor."

I applaud and praise the work of those individuals who have taken on the responsibility of translating Scripture so that we might have God's Word to study. However, we have to know that even the brightest and the best don't always come to a consensus. This explains why some translations include the comma and some do not. But either way, I think we can understand the meaning.

Now it's true that these days, we throw around the word *wonderful* for all kinds of situations that don't instill any real sense of wonder:

> "Jackson made the baseball team."
> "Wonderful!"
> "I'll be home for dinner after all."
> "Wonderful!"
> "Dad, I finally have enough for a down payment on
>   a new truck."
> "Wonderful!"

We've made the word very common, but there is NOTHING common about Jesus. Jesus is a real wonder. And He is wonderful.

Wonderful describes the coming One as incomprehensible, beyond understanding. *Wonderful* here is followed by *Counselor*. A counselor is one who advises, who gives counsel or instruction. The Wonderful Counselor as presented in this verse can be understood as a counselor who offers wisdom that is beyond common human understanding—advice that doesn't come from any everyday newspaper column or network talk-show host, or even from the most sage words of a highly respected scholar. This Counselor has wisdom to offer that is truly a wonder.

Jesus's wisdom was demonstrated early on, at the young age of twelve. His family had gone to Jerusalem for Passover. Then on the way home, they realized Jesus wasn't with the crowd. As a parent who has lost a child in a crowd, I ache from my toes to the top of my head. Mary and Joseph, Jesus's parents, rushed back to town. After looking all around, they went to the temple and there was Jesus, their twelve-year-old son, teaching. Luke described the scene: "All who heard him were amazed at his understanding and his answers" (Luke 2:47). And then again later, "Jesus grew in wisdom and in stature and in favor with God and all the people" (v. 52).

You might be thinking, *Of course He was wise. He was Jesus, the Son of God.* And that statement is true; however, Jesus was made flesh and dwelled among us (John 1:14). He was one of us, which is why His wisdom is also so wonderful for us now. He understands us like no one else.

Mighty God

Oh, the feathers that might fly in a scholarly roundtable discussion of the phrase "Mighty God." As I studied this, I found that for every two experts who agreed on a meaning, two more disagreed. The controversy doesn't seem to be with *gibbor*, which is the Hebrew word for "mighty," "strength," or "strong part." The rub seems to be with the title God, or *El* in Hebrew, being used here to describe the child to come. How could this child, this son to be given to us, also be God? How can Jesus be Father and Son? Ah, that's a great question, isn't it? So great, I called in an expert to fill in the blanks for us. Thank you, Charles Spurgeon, for leaving archives for us to study, because on this particular day we need them.

> The term here used for God, *El*, is taken from a Hebrew root, which, as I take it, signifies strength; and perhaps a literal translation even of that title might be, "The Strong one," the strong God. But there is added to this an adjective in the Hebrew, expressive of mightiness, and the two taken together express the omnipotence of Christ, his real deity and his omnipotence, as standing first and foremost among the attributes which the prophet beheld.... It does not say that Christ *shall be* "the mighty God,"—that is affirmed in many other places of Sacred Writ; but here it says, "He shall be *called* Wonderful," *called* "Counsellor," *called*, "The mighty God;" and I think that therefore I may be excused from entering into any proof of the fact, if I am at least able to establish the truth of that which is here foretold, inasmuch as Christ is indeed called at this day, and shall be called to the end of the world, "the mighty God."[2]

I'm not going to deny that many smart people have spoken into this piece of the prophecy. The bottom line for me is faith. Faith in the fact that Jesus is both God and man. How is this possible? How can this be? Even the smartest of the smart can't answer that. We either believe or we don't. As for me, I believe. By faith, I believe.

"Oh, how great are God's riches and wisdom and knowledge! How impossible it is for us to understand his decisions and his ways! For who can know the LORD's thoughts? Who knows enough to give him advice?" (Rom. 11:33–34). I don't have to have the Trinity fully defined—which is a blessing! Instead, I can focus on the undeniable evidence of God's greatness and consider His mighty power and what that means for me. It's enough for me to know that the God who is able to hold oceans in His hand and move mountains is the same God I can call on to hold my hand and stand with me through mountains of troubles.

Everlasting Father

I almost don't know how to enter this part of our conversation. If we were hanging out in my family room just chatting and the subject of fathers came up, each of us would have a different story to share. To some, the title *Father* brings warm and happy memories. Daddy coming to ball games and ballet recitals. Dad giving driving instructions and making sure we had a dollar tucked away for some gas and a quarter to call home in an emergency (before cell phones were a thing). To others, a father is nothing more than a genetic contributor. Maybe for them the word means someone who was supposed to be there but wasn't. A man of constant disappointment. Unreliable, perhaps even absent. And for still others, the word *father* might cause their heads to drop in sorrow because Daddy isn't living any longer and they miss him terribly every day.

So I tread lightly here, keeping in mind the tenderness of your heart. My intention isn't to stir up painful memories but to pour hope into those wounds by introducing you to a Father like no other.

The Messiah, Jesus, is our Everlasting Father. The Hebrew meaning of the phrase translates to "Father of eternity." The broader idea is that His fatherliness will not end. God will never not be a Father to us. (I realize I just sent all my English-teacher friends off the rail with the double negative.) Go ahead and take a moment to allow that to sink in. Forever, we have someone who will protect us from the mean girls at the lunchroom table. There is someone to look ahead over the horizon to see what we cannot see and who loves us enough to guide us in another direction. For eternity, there will be a safe place to go and cry; a person there to hear about the bullies at work, to complain to about our endless to-do list, and to assure us that everything will be okay.

Paul wrote about the fatherliness of God: "So you have not received a spirit that makes you fearful slaves. Instead, you received God's Spirit when he adopted you as his own children. Now we call him, 'Abba, Father'" (Rom. 8:15). Romans in the New Testament was originally written in Greek, with some words, like "Abba," coming from the Aramaic language. As you might have guessed from the sound of it, "Abba, Father" is an affectionate term, the kind of name a child makes up to call her father, like "Daddy" or "Papa." We who are children of God can talk to Him with the familiarity and closeness of a little girl sitting on her father's knee.

Regardless of your relationship with your earthly father, you need to know that you have a heavenly Father who is on your side, will never let you down, and will always love you. He knows your name and calls to you. He will never leave you. Just the thought of that brings me peace. How about you?

Prince of Peace

Peace. Hearing the word makes me want to inhale slowly, then exhale. My mind immediately brings up pictures of my favorite peaceful spot. What is your place of peace, your go-to refuge of rest? If I can't get there by car, I transport myself there in thought—the beach. The wind, the sound of the waves, the sand between my toes, and earbuds blasting praise music bring a calm to my chaos. Perhaps you're a mountain girl, rocking on the front porch of a cabin nestled in the woods by a singing creek. Or do you prefer driving on a quiet road, enjoying a steaming cup of something foaming at your favorite coffeehouse, or snuggling under warm blankets in your bed-pants and bingeing on sappy Hallmark movies? You've got a place; we all do. It's a place where we rush to escape from the crazy the world throws at us.

But you don't just have a place. You have a person.

Jesus is the Prince of Peace. The maker, dispenser, cultivator, and leader of peace. There are a few kinds of peace often referred to in Scripture. One is the peace of salvation, which reconciles or makes man right with God (2 Cor. 5:19). Another kind of peace is situational. It's the experience of calm and confident faith, even when we are in the chemo chair, the unemployment line, a prison cell, a courtroom, or a funeral home. Our desire would be for God to remove us from these places and keep us from ever having to go through these trials. However, these troubles are a result of a world that rejects God and of the sinful nature in our DNA.

Jesus spoke of peace in a conversation with His disciples, His closest friends, in John 14:27: "I am leaving you with a gift—peace of mind and heart. And the peace I give is a gift the world cannot give. So don't be troubled or afraid." We can be so grateful for our Friend like no other, who quiets our soul when the world spews ugliness, pain, and trouble. But will the world ever be absent of war, famine, disease, and sorrow? Can there be peace in this world? Oh, yes.

Jesus will come back, praise God! He will set up a perfect earthly kingdom. All war will cease, disease will be defeated, hunger will be satisfied, and sorrow will turn to joy. Until that happens, let's savor every moment in His presence, soaking in all the peace He offers.

The Path

We've studied the position and the person of Jesus; now let's follow the path from Isaiah's prophecy to you and me.

> For unto you is born this day in the city of David a Saviour, which is Christ the Lord.
> And this shall be a sign unto you; Ye shall find the babe wrapped in swaddling clothes, lying in a manger. (Luke 2:11–12 KJV)

I don't know what time of year you are reading *Jesus Everlasting*, but Jesus's birth is a refreshing story no matter what the season. I enjoy reading the story in the King James Version—it just has that poetic rhythm that makes my heart flutter. Do you agree?

Jesus was born in Bethlehem, also known as the City of David. He was the long-awaited Messiah (*Christ* means "Messiah" or "anointed one"), but He wasn't what anyone expected. While the prophecy about the child to come had been passed down from generation to generation, the Jews were expecting a political figure, someone raised in the culture and poised to take over and defend them against Rome. But instead they got a helpless, dependent baby, born to a common Jewish family in a lowly environment. His humble beginning seemed a lifetime away from the kind of ruling, reigning, and redeeming of the people that the Jewish leaders were looking for. The gift promised was the gift given, yet somehow not the gift wanted.

The Jews missed the fulfillment of this prophecy and others. Let's take a look at some of these Old Testament prophecies and the corresponding verses that represent their fulfillment.

Old Testament Prophecy

Fulfillment

All right then, the Lord himself will give you the sign. Look! The virgin will conceive a child! She will give birth to a son and will call him Immanuel (which means "God is with us"). (Isa. 7:14)

"How will this be," Mary asked the angel, "since I am a virgin?" (Luke 1:34 NIV)

But you, Bethlehem Ephrathah, though you are small among the clans of Judah, out of you will come for me one who will be ruler over Israel, whose origins are from of old, from ancient times. (Mic. 5:2 NIV)

After Jesus was born in Bethlehem in Judea, during the time of King Herod, Magi from the east came to Jerusalem. (Matt. 2:1 NIV)

And through your [Abraham's] offspring all nations on earth will be blessed, because you have obeyed me. (Gen. 22:18 NIV)

This is the genealogy of Jesus the Messiah the son of David, the son of Abraham. (Matt. 1:1 NIV)

Most Jews simply did not accept this gift, Jesus, as *the* Messiah, their Messiah. It seems puzzling with so much evidence, but we have the benefit of the entire canon of Scripture, something they did not. Isaiah and Jesus both spoke of a spiritual blindness that would come upon the people.

And he said, "Yes, go, and say to this people,

'Listen carefully, but do not understand.
　　Watch closely, but learn nothing.'
Harden the hearts of these people.
　　Plug their ears and shut their eyes.
That way, they will not see with their eyes,
　　nor hear with their ears,
nor understand with their hearts
　　and turn to me for healing." (Isa. 6:9–10)

Enter the Gentiles

Since God's people, the Jews, did not receive and accept Jesus, God empowered the disciples and equipped them through Jesus to extend the Abrahamic Covenant (Gen. 22:18) to the Gentiles (any non-Jews) and to anyone who would believe. "For God so loved the world, that he gave his only begotten Son, that whosoever believeth in him should not perish, but have everlasting life" (John 3:16 KJV). The account of Paul's commissioning to preach the good news of the gospel of Jesus to all people is recorded in Acts 9.

There are too many verses to share in our short time together supporting the invitation to all people to salvation. It is enough to say that the "us" in Isaiah's prophecy, "For a child is born to us, a son is given to us. The government will rest on his shoulders. And he will be called: Wonderful Counselor, Mighty God, Everlasting Father, Prince of Peace" (Isa. 9:6), now includes you and me and any other person in the whole world. In fact, why don't you circle, highlight, or underline "us"? How about writing "I am part of us" in the margin?

One last thing about the child: I do hope you noticed the child was given. We didn't deserve Him. We didn't earn Him.... He. Was. Given. Let that sink in. A gift is given. A gift has to be received. Now let's go see how we can unwrap and experience this gift every day.

Everlasting Thoughts

Remember, don't erase, edit, or omit. Just put pen or pencil to paper and listen to what God is trying to teach you through His Word right now.

Write out in a list the four names of the Son given to us from Isaiah 9:6. What will He be called?

Now beside each name in that list, write a name you can come up with that has a similar meaning. For example, for "Mighty God" I might say "Strong Ruler of Everything."

Remember the context we talked about for Isaiah and what was going on for the people at the time the prophet delivered his message. How do you think the people must have felt to hear about this hope to come? How does this message make you feel now?

Of the four character attributes of Jesus represented by the four names—wisdom, strength, faithfulness, and peace—which one stands out most to you as being something you long for right now?

Read 2 Corinthians 4:4:

> Satan, who is the god of this world, has blinded the minds
> of those who don't believe. They are unable to see the glori-
> ous light of the Good News. They don't understand this
> message about the glory of Christ, who is the exact likeness
> of God.

Imagine a path stretches out in front of you that leads straight to
Jesus. Is there anything on that path that is blocking your way to
get closer to Jesus today? If there is, pray and ask God to remove the
obstacles or distractions that are getting in your way. And if there
isn't, keep an eye out as we move forward in this story. Satan is tricky!
Ask God to help you keep your vision clear and your heart pure as
you seek to know Jesus more.

Leaning on the Music: "Amazing Grace"

Published in 1779, tune of "New Britain," words by John Newton

Amazing grace! (how sweet the sound)
That saved a wretch like me!
I once was lost, but now am found,
Was blind, but now I see.

Are you singing? It's okay. I'll admit that, after I typed the words, I paused to sing them ... more than once. "Amazing Grace" is perhaps one of the most well-known and beloved hymns of all times. The masterpiece has been updated with faster tempos and modernized instrumentals, but nothing can replace the hymn as I first learned it.

I know, talking about my love for hymns dates me, but I'm okay with that. I love all music that points me to my Creator. Hymns hold a special place in my heart, primarily in part because of Hymn Night. Once a quarter, our director of music would plan a Sunday evening service of only music. The congregation would call out the hymn number, we'd quickly turn to the page, then we'd all sing a verse followed by the chorus. It was so much fun!!

I had always, always, *always* wanted to shout out a hymn number. Finally, one Sunday, my trembling heart was brave enough to burst out a number—"188!" When the director acknowledged my outcry by telling the accompanist "188, 'Amazing Grace,'" I could hardly contain myself. My face feels flushed even now as I recall the moment. Boldly, I belted out:

> Amazing grace! (how sweet the sound)
> That saved a wretch like me!
> I once was lost, but now am found,
> Was blind, but now I see.

Even though I had made a profession of faith by my debut at Hymn Night, I didn't fully comprehend the impact of these words penned by John Newton. All these years later, God's saving grace still confounds me. Writer Justin Holcomb said, "Grace is the love of God shown to the unlovely; the peace of God given to the restless; the unmerited favor of God."[3] Jesus shows that grace to a lost and dying world that included me. I was a wretch separated from a holy God, but now, I am a sinner sanctified and cleansed by the selfless act of God and His Son, Jesus Christ.

Because of this sacrifice, those who are spiritually blind can now receive the gift of salvation; they can see the works of His hands and the wonder of His truths come alive in their lives. No one has to wander this world feeling lost and alone. He will find you. Oh, and the sound of grace is so sweet, you nearly lose your breath when you experience it. This grace goes beyond the cross of Christ and is extended to us every day.

Oh, how I marveled, and still do, at the first verse, and then celebrated the amazing grace of the final verse, as we used to sing it. This verse, as I discovered, was not the final verse in the original work by John Newton, as the other verses I knew were. It was instead added from a song titled "Jerusalem, My Happy Home." It first appeared in *Uncle Tom's Cabin*, by Harriet Beecher Stowe, as a verse sung by Uncle Tom. Honestly, typing the words even now overwhelms me:

> When we've been there ten thousand years
> Bright shining as the sun,
> We've no less days to sing God's praise
> Than when we first begun.

As if the gift of grace that saves and sustains wasn't enough, we have the grace of eternity. "188! 188!" I shouted that number out then, not even knowing that I would soon be belting out the truth of the gospel. Have you received the grace of salvation? If you aren't sure, you can pray right now: *Lord, I confess that I am a sinner in need of You to be my Savior. I believe Jesus died for my sins and rose again so that I might have eternal life. Will You come into my heart and save me? Thank You for Your amazing grace and for saving a wretch like me.*

Praise God for the blessed assurance of salvation through the gift of His amazing grace. And, friend, I will see you in heaven's choir. I wonder if the Director will take requests.

Chapter 2

A Counselor Who Knows Us

There's a guilty little secret I'm terribly embarrassed to admit to you, but I feel like as a friend you won't hold this against me. This *is* a judgment-free zone, right?

(Deep breath.)

From 1986 through about 2000, every afternoon at 4:00, you would find me planted on my couch watching *The Oprah Winfrey Show*. If I wasn't watching, I was recording it to watch later. (Does anyone remember those huge VHS tapes?) Yes, I was one of the millions of people, primarily women, who tuned in each day to receive a daily dose of Oprah. We learned our shoes should match the closest article of clothing to our feet and that sucking in our cheeks when applying bronzer would make it appear that we had high cheekbones. (Please tell me you've done that.) We watched as Hollywood's A-list debuted their most recent movies and as heartbroken couples tried to reconcile and find hope. However, as popular as her show grew to be, Oprah wasn't the pioneer in public self-help shows.

For centuries, we have been going public for advice and counsel. Women started seeking domestic advice about making biscuits and sewing on buttons as far back as the 1880s. "Dear Abby" became an influential advice column in the 1950s. Women moved from how-to homemaking counsel to relationship remedies, and making headway in the workplace. But the ink on the advice columns, though they were still widely popular, faded into the background with the invention of the television.

Many talk shows have spanned the decades since televisions first filled our homes, but none more noted than Phil Donahue. He was the real pioneer in the audience-participation show. For twenty-nine years, televisions across the country were tuned in for advice and insight on everything from politics to what used to be private matters. Oprah replaced Phil D., and Dr. Phil replaced Oprah. Dr. Phil McGraw became a regular guest on Oprah's show, appearing weekly as a relationship-strategy expert. This led to him having his own show. His eighteen seasons on the air have earned him awards and recognition for being the most well-known mental-health professional.

Please hear me. I'm not throwing Abby, Phil, Oprah, Dr. Phil, and all the other well-known and well-intentioned advisers under the bus. I don't even know how many mental-health professionals have some kind of podcast or reality show or TED Talk out there these days, but there must be hundreds, if not thousands. Of course, a lot of good has been done during the tenure of these notable folks: awareness of needs in the world around us has increased, families have been reunited, social depravity has been revealed and poised for remedy, and on some occasions, the name of Jesus has even been mentioned. However, all this free guidance and readily available expertise have caused us to tend to seek earthly sources of help from strangers first rather than turning to our heavenly Counselor, to the one person who knows us better than anyone else.

Seeking counsel from the world didn't start with Oprah or the "Happy Homemaker" newspaper column. The apostle Paul warned of this in his letter to Timothy: "For the time will come when they will not tolerate sound doctrine; but wanting to have their ears tickled, they will accumulate for themselves teachers in accordance with their own desires" (2 Tim. 4:3 NASB). The thirst for more knowledge and to hear what we want to hear was passed to us through our genetic code.

When God Became Not Enough

We have to travel way, way back; back to the very beginning, back to a time of perfection and complete unity with our Creator, long before television and print. We are off to Eden.

In the beginning God created the heavens and the earth. (Gen. 1:1)

So God created human beings in his own image.
In the image of God he created them;
male and female he created them. (v. 27)

Then God looked over all he had made, and he saw that it was very good!
And evening passed and morning came, marking the sixth day. (v. 31)

In the beginning God created the heavens, the earth, and everything in it, including man and woman. Please notice, and perhaps underline, the phrase in verse 31: "it was very good." It was good—all of it—until it wasn't. There was beauty, good food, and freedom. There was no sin and no shame. There was peace and open communication with God. God was in charge. Man and woman were subject to Him and it was good, until man and woman exchanged God's good for their own idea of good.

One day, someone told Eve that what God had given wasn't good … enough. He told her that she could have more. *More* wasn't part of God's design. He had given the man and woman everything they needed and it *was* enough.

✝ More *wasn't part of God's design.*

All they needed was in the garden, on the east side of Eden. God planted many trees, each uniquely beautiful. In the middle of the garden were two trees—the tree of life and the tree of the knowledge of good and evil (Gen. 2:9). Adam and Eve were given permission to enjoy all the things in the garden, except one tree. The tree of the knowledge of good and evil was just as beautiful as the others; however, it was forbidden, for God warned them, "If you eat its fruit, you are sure to die" (v. 17).

Although everything God created was good, and is good, not everything was designed for human consumption. To understand this better, let's turn to this ancient conversation that changed the course of history—the conversation that tickled Eve's ears and made her heart yearn for more.

> The serpent was the shrewdest of all the wild animals the LORD God had made. One day he asked the woman, "Did God really say you must not eat the fruit from any of the trees in the garden?"
>
> "Of course, we may eat fruit from the trees in the garden," the woman replied. "It's only the fruit from the tree in the middle of the garden that we are not allowed to eat. God said, 'You must not eat it or even touch it; if you do, you will die.'"
>
> "You won't die!" the serpent replied to the woman. "God knows that your eyes will be opened as soon as you eat it, and you will be like God, knowing both good and evil."
>
> The woman was convinced. She saw that the tree was beautiful and its fruit looked delicious, and she wanted the wisdom it would give her. So she took some of the fruit and ate it. Then she gave some to her husband, who was with her, and he ate it, too. (Gen. 3:1–6)

Good was no longer good, because Satan, disguised as a serpent, convinced the woman that what the good God had provided wasn't good *enough*. Yes, he lied and twisted God's words, but his argument compelled Eve to partake of the forbidden. His words led Eve to believe that she wasn't

- wise enough—he told her she could be wiser yet;
- fulfilled enough—he offered something that seemed more fulfilling;
- loved enough—because God didn't grant her access to everything; and
- strong enough—because God had more power than she did.

Oh, friend, the forbidden is always beautiful, and it will lead us to looking for more by convincing us that we don't have enough. Sin came into this world through one man (Rom. 5:12), and we've been fighting the pull ever since. Eve accepted counsel from someone who wasn't an expert on her life. And without realizing it, we have been following Eve's example ever since.

The Danger of Bad Counsel

It's been said that a hairdresser is a Christian woman's bartender: she listens to everything and gives good advice. Now let me be honest; I haven't received counsel from a bartender. In fact, to my knowledge, I've never spoken to a bartender. I do, however, speak to my hairstylist about every five weeks. And she normally does give good counsel … except that one time when she should have counseled me but didn't.

I'm not sure what had gotten into me, a wild hair of sorts. I showed up at my regular color appointment, and before I knew it, some words had come tumbling out of my mouth. Now, for the record, trouble usually follows the sentence "I want to do something *different*." And so, with a notion in my mind unaccompanied by discernment, I suggested to my stylist that I might look good with a blonde streak on the part of my hair that swooshed over the right side of my face.

Without much discussion, she hurried to the back to mix the blonding-color cocktail. It wasn't until after the shampoo, rinse, and style that I gagged on my words. Hairstyle change really should be prayed over, girlfriends, just saying. And it should *never* be made while under the influence of hormonal duress.

We laugh about it still to this day … the day I went off the range. Yes, she still styles my hair. A girl doesn't give up on the ten-year investment of a stylist-client relationship because of one color situation gone bad. (And all the hairstylists say, "Amen.")

Bad counsel can lead to bad hair, which is a temporary condition. On a much greater scale, permanent damage can be the result of poor advice. Let's take Eve, for instance. All the world's undesirable situations can be traced back to the day when good went bad and she listened to bad counsel. Sin, the knowledge of good and evil, and the desire to have godlike wisdom were all introduced to the world. This event allowed Satan to cross the threshold of every heart. His ways worked then, and they work now (more on that later). For centuries Satan has been convincing us, just like he convinced Eve, that we need *more*.

The moment Adam and Eve ate the fruit, they realized they wanted more … clothes. They had the knowledge that they were naked and desired to be covered. With this realization, shame entered their world. God's response to Adam and Eve is priceless: "Who told you that you were naked?" (Gen. 3:11). We could ask ourselves the very same thing. Who told you things in your life don't measure up? Who told you the pains of your past determine the direction of your future? Who told you that you don't have enough?

When we allow voices that don't come from Jesus or from people who live by His truths to speak into our lives, we will be led away from the Wonderful One, our every-day, very own, personal Wonderful Counselor.

> † *For centuries Satan has been convincing us, just like he convinced Eve, that we need more.*

The apostle Paul candidly wrote to Timothy, giving a warning about the last days, about individuals who will tell us these things and influence us to live in a way contrary to God's way. His words cut to the quick and shift our gaze from the Wonderful One to our own lives. Brace yourself. This truth is hard to hear.

> But understand this, that in the last days there will come times of difficulty. For people will be lovers of self, lovers of money, proud, arrogant, abusive, disobedient to their parents, ungrateful, unholy, heartless, unappeasable, slanderous, without self-control, brutal, not loving good,

treacherous, reckless, swollen with conceit, lovers of pleasure rather than lovers of God, having the appearance
of godliness, but denying its power. Avoid such people.
(2 Tim. 3:1–5 ESV)

Grab your pen or highlighter to emphasize "Avoid such people."
Such people lead us away from the Wonderful Counselor who has
authority to speak into and lead our lives. Now I know what you're
thinking, because I thought it too. *I would never allow them around
me. Avoiding such people will be absolutely no problem for me. I go to
church, read my Bible, and obey God.* As I said, brace yourself.

For among them are those who creep into households and
capture weak women, burdened with sins and led astray by
various passions, always learning and never able to arrive at
a knowledge of the truth. (vv. 6–7 ESV)

Yeah, I know. These verses can hurt a Jesus girl's feelings, or at
the very least, make the hair on the back of her neck stand up. Let's
address that *w*-word right away—the one that comes right before
"women." Oh, I wish I could share a synonym that softens the sug-
gestion of the word, but I can't. Some translations use the words
gullible or *vulnerable*; another uses the word *silly*. None of these
words surround you with love and warmth. They cut to the core.
In the original language the word means "weak-willed."[1] But rather
than getting sideways and taking the language Paul used as a personal
insult, why don't we sit up straight in our chairs like real women and
take in this warning.

We have to admit it; there is truth here. *Such people* do creep into our homes when we choose to read a grocery-store magazine article about saving our marriage rather than consulting our Bibles. *Such people* speak into our lives each time we turn on the television to watch a show whose standards don't align with God's Word. The songs and podcasts we tune in to influence our thinking. All these voices can make us weak and vulnerable to the enemy.

> ✝ It doesn't take long to get lost and confused about what is true.

We may expand our listening and reading to help us know what is going on in the culture; however, culture can take root and replace faith. The lines between acceptable and unacceptable become blurred. The answers that used to be biblically black and white turn gray. The more cultural voices infiltrate our lives, the more we believe the things they teach and advise. Slowly, without awareness, our standards change; the bar is lowered. Our faith weakens as we become lovers of self, lovers of money, proud, arrogant, abusive, disobedient to parents, ungrateful, unholy, heartless, unappeasable, slanderous, without self-control, brutal, not loving good, treacherous, reckless, swollen with conceit, lovers of pleasure rather than lovers of God, people having the appearance of godliness, but denying its power. When we live this way, we go to the wrong places and ask the wrong people to help us navigate life's bumps and turns. It doesn't take long to get lost and confused about what is true and where truth can be found.

So what's a woman who has succumbed to *such people* to do? How does a woman burdened with sins, led astray by various passions, always learning and unable to arrive at a knowledge of the truth find the Wonderful Counselor? Don't worry; He'll find you, even if He has to go through Samaria.

The One Who Had to Go

It's really hard to get lost these days. With phone apps like Google Maps, Waze, and Maps.me, we get to where we are going, even if we've never been there before. "Lola" (the name I've given the voice on my phone that helps me) talks to me when I travel. She warns me when trouble is ahead, alerts me as I approach or accidently miss a turn, and assures me when I am on the fastest route to my destination. Doesn't everyone want to make good time by taking the quickest roads? Of course we do. But what if the fastest passage isn't the most desired way?

Jesus often took unexpected routes to get His message across. One day, one of these routes led Him through an area where men like Him, Jewish men, would not normally choose to go.

He left Judea and returned to Galilee.

It was necessary for Him to go through Samaria. (John 4:3–4 AMPC)

He left Judea and returned to Galilee.

He had to go through Samaria on the way. (John 4:3–4 NLT)

Yes, I realize the same scripture is listed twice, but I'm nerdy like that. Why use one translation to teach your point when you can use two? Will you underline or highlight *had to* and *necessary*. Scholar William Mounce gave the meaning of these words from the Greek in this way: "it is a must, it is necessary (one should, ought)."[2]

Jesus had been doing ministry. He and His disciples were hungry and ready to move on, so to avoid potential political trouble in Jerusalem, they decided to head to Galilee. A physical need motivated the disciples; however, Jesus was moved by a spiritual need. A woman who lived in Samaria was in need of spiritual nourishment. If Jesus had used my Google Maps, Lola would have assured Him that He was on the fastest route yet alerted Him to the situation at Jacob's well. Regardless of the alert, Jesus would have kept going, because He couldn't *not* go … it was necessary.

It all sounds simple enough. A woman needed Jesus—He went to meet her. However, it wasn't that easy-peasy. The choice to take this route to Galilee was actually a controversial one. But Jesus will go to any length to introduce himself to someone in need.

Jesus was a Jew, and long-standing contention existed between the Jews and Samaritans. The conflict started when Babylon conquered the southern kingdom of Judah and left the lowest-class citizens behind. Non-Jewish people migrated into the region and began to intermarry, mixing beliefs, superstitions, and customs. The result? The Samaritans. When the exiles returned from captivity, they found this new, half-Jewish people group living in their home-land. Jews (in general) despised them and referred to Samaritans as "half-breeds."

Knowing this tidbit of history helps us understand the impact of the word *necessary*. The Jews typically used the longer route, beyond the Jordan, when traveling to Galilee, so as to avoid any encounters with the Samaritans. However, there was one Jew who *had to* go through Samaria. He crossed political, economic, and racial bound-aries to get to the one who needed Him. That's what Jesus does. He seeks and saves the lost (Luke 19:10) and leaves the ninety-nine to find the one (Matt. 18:12–14).

The One Who Had to Be Seen

Who is this one, this woman Jesus had to see? She was a woman who needed to meet Jesus.

- Scripture says she went late in the day to fetch water from the well. It was "about noontime" (John 4:6). Midday. Hot. The part of the day when women were inside in the cool of their homes tending to domestic duties, not out trek-king to the well.
- Scripture says she was alone (v. 7). A woman. Alone. Friendless. The other women in the com-munity most likely came to the well together to fetch water, but not her. Makes you wonder why, right?

- Scripture suggests that she wasn't a woman of means. She "came to draw water" herself (v. 7). That tells us that she was probably economically challenged. And most likely childless. Women of means, or those who had young handmaidens, never retrieved water for their own households. The younger, stronger women of the home would go to the well instead.

If anyone needed wisdom and guidance for her day, it was this woman, whose name we don't even know. She is known to us only as "the woman at the well" or "the Samaritan woman." The circumstances surrounding her suggest that she was *that* woman—you know, the one small-town gossips love to talk about. Fodder for every female fellowship. The one who causes us to cover our mouths when we talk so no one can read our lips. Yes, this was the one Jesus *had to* see. The one who needed to see Him.

As the story unfolds, it becomes obvious why she needed good counsel. Her lifestyle suggested she had been misguided somewhere along the way. She went off course. She had become weak-willed, burdened with sin, led astray by various passions, always learning yet unable to arrive at a knowledge of the truth … until this day, a day that started out like every other day, but ended like no other.

The Counselor Counsels

A counselor has to be a skilled conversationalist. He or she must have the gift of gab and the ability to not only start a dialogue but also maintain the dialogue when the enviable awkward moment of silence screams. A therapist intentionally phrases his or her responses in a way that draws out the desired response from deep within the person. Another counseling technique is to ask questions. The questions are probing and open in nature, and don't necessarily have right or wrong answers. A good counselor uses these conversational methods to help a client facilitate self-evaluation, which enables one to discover the source of a problem. Further, a Christian counselor asks questions and directs the client to the Bible as the source of advice and guidance.

A counselor's questions might be irritating and sound more like an interrogation than therapy. However, questions help us find answers. They may unearth hurt, incite anger, or awaken emotions that were once buried. However, what is revealed enables us to rise up and move forward. On this particular day, the woman was moving toward the well for water, completely unaware she was moving toward a freedom she'd never known yet always longed for.

Let's look in on the conversation between the woman and Jesus through the lens of a counselor (John 4:7–15). If you can, read it out loud.

> Jesus said to her, "Please give me a drink." He was alone at the time because his disciples had gone into the village to buy some food.
>
> The woman was surprised, for Jews refuse to have anything to do with Samaritans. She said to Jesus, "You are a Jew, and I am a Samaritan woman. Why are you asking me for a drink?"

Jesus replied, "If you only knew the gift God has for you and who you are speaking to, you would ask me, and I would give you living water."

"But sir, you don't have a rope or a bucket," she said, "and this well is very deep. Where would you get this living water? And besides, do you think you're greater than our ancestor Jacob, who gave us this well? How can you offer better water than he and his sons and his animals enjoyed?"

Jesus replied, "Anyone who drinks this water will soon become thirsty again. But those who drink the water I give will never be thirsty again. It becomes a fresh, bubbling spring within them, giving them eternal life."

"Please, sir," the woman said, "give me this water! Then I'll never be thirsty again, and I won't have to come here to get water."

Jesus is the master counselor, isn't He? Wow. Without saying anything disrespectful, He rattled the woman's soul. She wanted what He was offering. Perhaps she was tired of facing the ridicule and stares every day, not to mention the scorching heat and that long, lonely walk to the well. But the woman was thinking logically, not spiritually: "Then I'll never be thirsty again, and I won't have to come here to get water." She wanted Jesus to improve her life without inconveniencing her.

A good Christian counselor works with us to reveal our needs while pointing us to God's Word as the source of satisfaction and healing. This woman recognized her practical needs, but not her spiritual ones. Jesus, her Wonderful Counselor, would stay with her until her spirit understood and her soul received His gift.

The water she *thought* she needed was temporary, would run out, and cause her to come back to the well every day. She would have understood the term *living water*, as all those living in the region would, as running water—the underground water source that supplied the well.

Jesus, however, was speaking of a spiritual source of refreshment. The wise One (performing the job of a good counselor) used this play on words to make the woman think. The water He was talking about would never run out, would satisfy her every need, and in fact, would overflow from her, making others thirsty for it. *Hudór záō* was the living water Jesus was speaking of in John 4:10 when He said to her, "If you only knew the gift God has for you … I would give you living water." *Thayer's Greek Lexicon* defines *záō* as "bubbling up, gushing forth, flowing." The idea of this flowing water was a metaphor for the living spirit and truth of God. Water in cisterns or pools is still and becomes stagnant, but flowing water comes from a source that gets continually replenished, so the water is pure and continues to provide refreshment.[3] I love Bible commentator David Guzik's thoughts about this living water: "The effect of this water does much more than simply satisfy the thirst of the one who drinks it. It also creates something good, something life-giving in the heart of the one who drinks it.… It *becomes* a fountain of water springing up into everlasting life."[4] Now I ask, who wouldn't want this kind of water?

But the Samaritan woman's tone quickly became argumentative and defensive as she spoke to this man she didn't know. Isn't the same true of you and me when certain things are said a certain way? Our ears itch to hear what we want to hear, and when we hear something we don't like, we become agitated. He left her thirsting for more. Let's eavesdrop on more of their conversation (vv. 16–18).

"Go and get your husband," Jesus told her.
"I don't have a husband," the woman replied.

Ouch. (He called her out.)

Jesus said, "You're right! You don't have a husband—for you have had five husbands, and you aren't even married to the man you're living with now. You certainly spoke the truth!"

This Wonderful Counselor saw right through her. She was exposed. The source of the problem had been identified. The words about her past and present relationships most assuredly hit her like a splash of cold well water. Perhaps she even had to grab hold of the edge of the well to maintain her balance as she desperately attempted to process all that had just been revealed. I imagine she breathed deeply as questions raced through her mind: *How does He know this about me? Is all this even possible? What is He talking about? I can have the needs and desires of my heart satisfied? Me? It won't matter what I've done or what others say about me?*

The woman and the Counselor continued to banter back and forth. She validated His wealth of knowledge but got in over her head (like most of us do when we start trying to tell the Lord His business) the minute she started talking about worshipping on the mountains. Jesus wowed her with more prophetic words. Let's listen in to the conversation from verses 19–25:

> "Sir," the woman said, "you must be a prophet. So tell me, why is it that you Jews insist that Jerusalem is the only place of worship, while we Samaritans claim it is here at Mount Gerizim, where our ancestors worshiped?"
>
> Jesus replied, "Believe me, dear woman, the time is coming when it will no longer matter whether you worship the Father on this mountain or in Jerusalem. You Samaritans know very little about the one you worship, while we Jews know all about him, for salvation comes through the Jews. But the time is coming—indeed it's here now—when true worshipers will worship the Father in spirit and in truth. The Father is looking for those who will worship him that way. For God is Spirit, so those who worship him must worship in spirit and in truth."
>
> The woman said, "I know the Messiah is coming—the one who is called Christ. When he comes, he will explain everything to us."

I find it so interesting that she knew about Jesus. She knew the Messiah was coming but couldn't recognize Him standing right in front of her. Our Counselor revealed himself at just the right time.

As the woman attempted to end the conversation, Jesus himself stopped the show with a one-liner to beat all one-liners (I hope you are sitting down for this): "I AM the Messiah!" (v. 26).

Drop the mic and close the curtain. *I AM.* Words of comfort and words of conviction. She finally knew who He was, and most importantly, she knew who *she* was—a woman redeemed. Her life had intersected with the Savior of the universe. If she hadn't invested herself in the conversation, being willing to hear and accept the hard stuff, she would have walked away with a full jug of water but an empty soul. She would have gone back home and continued to allow the enemy to convince her that she wasn't wise, fulfilled, loved, or strong enough because God didn't grant her everything. She made the right choice, and many people were splashed by the living water bubbling up from her.

> The woman left her water jar beside the well and ran back to the village, telling everyone, "Come and see a man who told me everything I ever did! Could he possibly be the Messiah?" So the people came streaming from the village to see him. (vv. 28–30)

We may not know her name, but we know who she was—the first female evangelist. She was the first woman to tell others about the saving grace of Jesus Christ. And God took her testimony and transformed lives.

Time Well Spent

Oh, one last thing: please notice with me that the woman *left her water jar*! In fact, highlight or underline that phrase. When you've been in the presence of Jesus, you just aren't that thirsty for the things of this world anymore. The woman of Samaria left more than her jug behind. She walked away from the past she thought would always have a grip on her. She left the weight of her jar and the heaviness of the shame she carried every day as she walked to and from Jacob's well. Then she walked into a future she never dreamed possible. The woman could leave behind what she came to get, because she had received everything she needed from Jesus. Time spent with the Wonderful One, the Counselor, is always time well spent.

Years ago, I carried my water jug all over to the wells of the world wanting to be validated, fulfilled, satisfied, heard, and appreciated. The wells of shopping, soap operas, socializing, and serving in church. I would walk away full but shortly after would be parched again. It wasn't until I started investing in time with Jesus, reading God's Word, and submitting to what the Spirit, the Counselor, wanted to do in my life that I began to understand what this woman experienced that hot day at the well in Samaria.

God loved us enough to send His Son for us. Jesus loved us enough to die on the cross so we could live eternally. And the Spirit loves us enough to tell us the truth. Only someone who really loves you and knows you tells the truth, even if the truth will temporarily hurt.

We often go looking for a better well. We measure our value by the number of likes on our social media posts, our friend counts on Facebook, and followers on Instagram. We determine our knowledge by the number of degrees on our walls or dollars in our bank account. But the wells of the world will always leave you dry.

Our Wonderful Counselor, the Holy Spirit, who dwells in the life of every believer, is better than any well. He's a river deep and wide, flowing endlessly with mercy, grace, love, knowledge, wisdom, and counsel. Our Wonderful Counselor is the water we've all been looking for. Conversations with Him will cause us to be honest about our weaknesses, inspire us to grow in our faith, and propel us in the direction of His will for our lives. When we spend time with Jesus Everlasting, we will learn that we are

- wise women who can become wiser through our study of His Word;
- fulfilled women who have so much to give others;
- loved women, not because of what we do or have, but because of what has been done and given for us; and
- strong women who have been empowered by the riches of the God of the universe.

You may be thinking, *I've been to that well and tasted some of that living water. I tried, but it wasn't long before I was thirsty again.* Well, friend, try again. The thing is, we don't know how many times that Samaritan woman had heard about the love of God before she met Jesus that day. She obviously knew something about prophecy and worship and spiritual matters. But somehow, she hadn't had that personal connection with the one and only God. Somehow, she kept getting distracted by her need to be loved and provided for. But on that day, she took a risk. She spoke to a stranger, who just happened to be the most Wonderful Counselor, more wonderful than any therapist she could have ever found in the Samaritan LinkedIn app. She didn't run away from Him—not even when it got messy. She stayed and listened and asked and received answers.

So drink again. The more time you spend with Him, drinking the living water, the more you'll want. You might be surprised—a little sip on Sunday morning will no longer satisfy. Because Jesus isn't a onetime event—He is Jesus Everlasting. Jesus for Every Day. Jesus Always. Jesus On and On.

Everlasting Thoughts

Remember, don't erase, edit, or omit. Just put pen or pencil to paper and listen to what God is trying to teach you through His Word right now.

Get ready. You can't answer "the Bible" or "God." And you should try to answer with the first thing that comes to mind. Ready? What is your go-to place for advice? Who do you call when you need some good counsel?

Okay, now keep that person, place, or thing in mind. Think back to the last time you went there for counsel. Were you satisfied? For how long?

Remember in John 4:16, when Jesus said to the woman, "Go and get your husband"? And we all felt her swallow hard with a gulp before she answered Him? What would be the thing Jesus might say to you that would make you gulp and squirm? What truth about your life are you trying to conceal from Him?

How much do you relate to the idea of not feeling like enough—not wise enough, fulfilled enough, loved enough, or strong enough? Dig deeper and pick which one of these "not enough" feelings resonates most with you right now. Why?

When the woman told the people what Jesus had said to her, the people came to hear Him too. And they told the woman, "Now we believe, not just because of what you told us, but because we have heard him ourselves. Now we know that he is indeed the Savior of the world" (John 4:42). Because this one woman opened herself up to Jesus, listened to Him, and took His Word as truth, a whole village was changed. Dream big for a minute. What do you think might happen if you spent more time with the Wonderful Counselor and told people what He has done for you?

Read Romans 8:37–39. Whatever you think might be keeping you from drinking from the water Jesus offers, just know this today—there is nothing in this world or out of it that can separate you from the love of Jesus. Not one thing. That's how much He loves you. You can leave your jar behind and follow Him. Write "leave my jar" in a place where you can see it every day: on your phone or your bathroom mirror or wherever else your eyes might fall on it often (not behind the couch—no one wants to look back there). Remember that you don't have to keep seeking elsewhere for answers—Jesus Everlasting has the answers you are looking for.

Leaning on the Music: "You Changed My Name"

Words and music by Travis Cottrell, 2005

You met my dear friend Kristi at the beginning of the book. It was this precious soul who introduced me to in-depth Bible study. She taught me to pray without ceasing, to stand firm in the face of extreme adversity, to forgive those who have trespassed against me, and she demonstrated what it looks like to walk closely with the Good Shepherd. Our hearts are woven tightly by intercessory prayer, the love of God's Word, and worship. Our hearts also celebrate and are awed by our Savior through music, especially the worship songs of Travis Cottrell.

His recordings range from an a cappella rendition of "Be Thou My Vision" to dance-in-the-aisle fast tunes like "Ain't No Grave." He hasn't abandoned the beauty of a hymn, yet he has the gift of writing modern worship songs that grab your heart. One such song seized my heart back in 2005.

I had decided to be rebaptized, not because I didn't think the first one was valid, but because I had fallen in love with God anew.

There was a fresh wind and fire of the Holy Spirit consuming me. Making this transformation public was nonnegotiable. However, along with the new fervor came a renewed attack from the enemy. You see, my faith had been dormant, and I felt ineffective in the kingdom of God. My awakening ticked Satan off. When we take a stand in our faith, Satan stands against us. He began to undermine my new commitment with his old schemes. His best weapon against me? Insecurity. Then my insecurity met "You Changed My Name" by Travis Cottrell, and like he wrote in the song, "I['d] never be the same."

Through the words of this song, I was able to fully embrace my identity as a child of God. God changed me when He called me "forgiven" and "redeemed." He took away all my shame and wrote a new beginning to the old story I had been living.

Those who have been saved by the precious blood of the Lamb now walk in the light of His redeeming love. Sometimes we have to fight for the confidence; we have a relentless enemy whose sole purpose is to keep his foot on the scale of each of our lives—to weigh us down with our past. But the Lord God set the heart of every believer apart from our past and freed our souls from the enslaving power of shame. Our sin has been erased. Condemnation has no place in our hearts.

When the woman walked to the well, her name was Condemned, Unrighteous, Unclean, Defeated, Broken, and Bound. But Jesus changed all of that. In a few short minutes, and through a rather uncomfortable conversation, Jesus changed her name. Who she was before didn't matter anymore. He not only gave her a new name, but He endowed her with a new life.

As she dropped her water jug and ran to the village, the chains of her past fell off. His amazing grace set her free. He changed her name! From that day forward, she was called Redeemed, Restored, Victorious, Pure, and Free.

My dear, precious friend, the same Jesus who changed her name and my name has changed your name. Walk confidently in the light of His redeeming love, believing who you are in Christ. Oh, please allow Him to write a new ending to the story that you've been living.

Chapter 3

A Defender Who Stands with Us

The transition from elementary school to junior high causes most twelve-year-olds to shake in their Levi's. Wait a minute. Let me back the bus up to the schoolhouse. Once upon time, Levi's were the jeans of choice, and middle school was called junior high. Yeah, I'm *that* old. Anyway, no matter what you call it, the transition from a lower school to an upper school is hard. In one school you are the big fish in a small pond; in the other you are a small fish in a big pond. This was my situation back in nineteen seventy-something. I was nervous, but knowing that I had friends who would also be making the pilgrimage with me eased my anxiety.

Like the beginning of most school years, seventh grade started off exciting. New colored folders, filled with lined paper and tabbed labels bearing my class name, were all placed neatly in my Trapper Keeper. I had a good supply of freshly sharpened pencils, Ticonderoga of course. And I had a new lunch box, without anything on it, because character lunch boxes were *so* elementary school. Days were filled with giggling with my girlfriends (who had really "matured" over the summer), pointing at boys across the cafeteria, wrestling with the combination lock on my locker, and complaining about all the work we had to do. All in all it was normal, until a boy in my science class asked me for some gum.

The boy, whom I won't identify, was an acquaintance from elementary school. (He had changed a lot over the summer too.) As we sat and waited for class to begin, he asked me for a piece of gum. It was a logical question, because I was chewing gum a friend had given me. Politely I responded, "I don't have any gum." He didn't like my answer. He turned his whole body in front of me so no one could see him pull his knife and hold it up to me and demand, between his gritted teeth and clenched jaw, a piece of gum. Within seconds the bell rang, and our teacher entered the room from his hall-duty post to start the day's lesson. Needless to say, I didn't hear a word in Earth Science that day.

When the bell rang to indicate the class change, I quickly gathered my things and rushed to my next class, which was fortunately homeroom, and my teacher was a woman. I remember shifting from one foot to another as I waited patiently to speak to her. Everything was cloudy and moving in slow motion. *Did what just happen really happen? He wouldn't do that. He knows me. He was only joking. He's such a kidder.* Then I remembered the look in his eyes and the proximity of his body to mine. *Oh, yes, it really happened!* Nausea fell over me as I fumbled to find the words to tell my teacher what had happened.

Most everything is a blur from that point on: investigation of the incident, parent meeting with the principal, the boy suspended from school for a week—yes, only a week—and transferred out of any class we had together. I was left with sleepless nights full of nightmares. My parents refused to send me back to that school and made an appeal to the school board for a midyear transfer to a school closer to my home. The appeal was accepted, with the understanding that my parents would have to provide transportation since the new school was not in my district. Without hesitation, my parents agreed to the terms. The matter was over, but my nightmares weren't.

Recalling the moment-by-moment account of that event still leaves my mouth dry and a lump in my throat. Fear still rushes through my body, heating me from head to toe. It truly was one of the most terrifying moments of my life.

But above all the bad memories, I remember the awesome presence of my daddy.

Like many girls, I was, and as of the writing of this book still am, the light of my daddy's life. He loves his children fiercely. When the incident occurred, my daddy and my momma were like a lion and lioness on the prowl, ready to pounce on anyone who didn't believe me or wouldn't help me immediately. They were my true advocates through the entire ordeal. However, when the lights went out at night, Momma kissed me good night and my daddy lay on top of the covers right beside me until I feel asleep. He was a lion in my defense, and I was a lamb in his tender care. He had stood with me against my fears and he stayed with me. I've never had to wonder if Daddy would be there for me. Even today, as I sit miles from home in my quiet writing place, I know he would find a way to help me if I needed it.

> ✝ *He was a lion in my*
> *defense, and I was a lamb*
> *in his tender care.*

Some of you reading my words might feel angry or envious, because your earthly father was not such a good defender. Maybe he even abandoned or abused you. Your heart longs for a daddy who will lie right beside you at night until you fall asleep and take on the enemies of your day. My heart is so sensitive to those who have had a disappointing relationship with an earthly father. I'd love to hold the hand of my sister who stood center stage at the ballet recital frantically looking for that face among the other parents, who found no gift from Dad under the tree, and who received no birthday card in the mail. I want every one of you to discover the love of a Savior, a Daddy, a Defender, who will never let you down. Our God is mighty to save you for eternity in heaven with Him and to take on every enemy who tries to take you down. His defense will provide a security you've never known. He is the Mighty God who fights for you and stands with you when you feel defenseless, brokenhearted, and broken down.

Perspective on the Battle

Perspective is the ability to see all the relevant data in a meaningful relationship. In order for us to scratch the surface of who our Mighty

God is and the battles He fights on our behalf, we need to travel up, up to the heavens to gather relevant data in order to establish the relationship between God, Jesus, and *the* battle. Where exactly has the battle line been drawn? To understand the battle, we first have to recognize who is doing the fighting—who is on which side. Who is our enemy? Let's take a closer look.

Satan was once an angel who lived in heaven with God. If you've never heard this before, I know this might be incredibly hard to believe, but it's true. In a prophetic word, the prophet Ezekiel admonished the King of Tyre for his wickedness and evil, and the message directly points to the source of the king's evil as Satan:

> You were in Eden,
> the garden of God.
> Your clothing was adorned with every precious
> stone—
> red carnelian, pale-green peridot, white
> moonstone,
> blue-green beryl, onyx, green jasper,
> blue lapis lazuli, turquoise, and emerald—
> all beautifully crafted for you
> and set in the finest gold.
> They were given to you
> on the day you were created. (Ezek. 28:13)

Satan was beautiful. The prophet also spoke of his beauty—"You were the model of perfection, full of wisdom and exquisite in beauty" (v. 12)—as well as his authority—"I ordained and anointed you as the mighty angelic guardian. You had access to the holy mountain of God and walked among the stones of fire" (v. 14).

So what went so wrong? A beautiful angel that God created and trusted with authority went rogue. And then one day ...

> Your heart was filled with pride
> > because of all your beauty.
> Your wisdom was corrupted
> > by your love of splendor.
> So I threw you to the ground
> > and exposed you to the curious gaze
> > > of kings. (v. 17)

Jesus also spoke of Satan's exit from heaven. In Luke 10:18 we read, "'Yes,' he told them, 'I saw Satan fall from heaven like lightning!'" Satan, once in the splendor of the heavenlies, clothed in brilliance, full of authority, was pushed (I prefer this synonym) out of heaven because he became prideful. He wanted to dethrone God but instead was given a quick shove. The result is a jacked-up angel, bent on overtaking heaven; and if it means taking out God's people, he's all for it. You see, the battle started in heaven, continued in the garden, but ended on the cross.

Jesus defeated death, the punishment for all sin (Rom. 6:23). He bore the sin of all mankind on the cross (1 Pet. 2:24) and rose victorious, ending the battle between life and death (John 11:25–26). Death was emptied of its power. "Because God's children are human beings—made of flesh and blood—the Son also became flesh and blood. For only as a human being could he die, and only by dying could he break the power of the devil, who had the power of death"

(Heb. 2:14). Though his power has been crushed, Satan is unyielding in his pursuit to wreck our lives and mess with us until Jesus returns to take us home. God drew the battle line in heaven, Satan crossed it, and Jesus won it. We can all say "Glory, hallelujah" and do a Jesus dance!

Now wait a minute—I hear you. I hear you saying, "I don't feel like dancing much right now." You've got struggles that are weighing you down, stealing your joy, and tapping every ounce of your energy. I get it. Remember what we just noted: Satan is unyielding. He wants to keep you from dancing in glory. That's why it's so important to keep the proper perspective. These battles are never really about just us and what we want or need. Satan hates God. He uses us to get at God. We think it is about the job, the promotion, the child we desire, the husband we long for, or financial stress. We are under the illusion our battles are about something keeping us from a better house, more friends, and better health. That we should be cancer-free, debt-free, and disaster-free. Oh, friend, our perspective is all wrong.

> ✝ *Where you sit affects*
> *what you see.*

All these things are part of this world, a sin-soaked world. Yet this world is not our home. The battles we face are small inconveniences compared to our coming glory with the Strong One, our Hero, our Mighty God. Hear my heart please, friend. I know cancer, RA, MS, dementia, Alzheimer's, paraplegia, AIDS, and all the cruel illnesses and evils of this world are serious, hurtful, and heartbreaking. I have loved ones who struggle with them, so I am not, by any means, minimizing their effects. I'm not saying any of your personal struggles are trivial. And I'm certainly not saying there is anything wrong with caring about them. Remember—I'm the girl who switched schools and had nightmares because a boy threatened me over chewing gum. The burdens we deal with in this life—small, medium, or large—are real and can be scary for a moment or scarring for a lifetime. But here's the real problem: Satan uses the pains of this world to disrupt our immeasurably more living, to make us doubt God's eternal plan, and to distract us from kingdom work.

He's crafty. He places obstacles in our paths and then offers us a supposedly easy way out. He tries to trick us into thinking this world has something better to offer, when all the while he knows he has nothing for us. He is the defeated foe trying desperately to rack up some trophies. But the war is really between life and death; eternal union with God or eternal separation from God. The choice of which side of the battle line to live on is up to every individual. For me, the decision has been made: I stand on the side of the winner, Jesus.

You might be asking though, *If the ultimate battle has been won, and God is our Mighty God who fights for His children, then why do I have battle fatigue? I mean, if God is doing the fighting, why am I so tired?* I think it goes back to perspective. God sees our lives in light of eternity, and we see our lives in light of the temporary. His view is vertical, while our view is horizontal. Where you sit affects what you see. What you see determines your focus. And what you focus on is often where you aim your energy. We experience rest as we learn to focus on Him instead and trust Him with the battle. After all, His view is much clearer than ours. He sees from above.

A View from Above

I have so much respect for the men and women who serve in the armed forces. In times of peace, they are poised and ready. When the call comes to stand up and ship out, they go with allegiance and honor. And they trust their leaders to give them well-thought-out orders. To provide those orders, the commanders have to gather and verify intel, draw up strategic plans, and issue the orders. They have to view the battle not just from the ground but from above as well.

In the heavenly realm there is One who gives the orders. His name is Jehovah Sabaoth, which means Lord of Hosts or, in military terms, the Commander in Chief.

Yahweh-Sabaoth, Lord of Hosts (or Lord of Heaven's Armies), is mentioned over 250 times in the Old Testament. This title tells us the Lord is the commander of heaven and all the inhabitants of the earth, regardless of ethnicity, economic status, or geographical location. He has power, majesty, and authority to accomplish everything for everyone at any time. He sits on His throne and oversees what is happening everywhere all at once. The sovereign LORD of hosts—the only one in charge of heaven's armies of angels—has the grace to always be there for anyone who comes to Him through faith in the Lord Jesus Christ. The King of Glory, who commands His armies in the heavens and on the earth, will eventually defeat all His enemies in this world. He is Jesus Christ.[1]

There isn't anything going on with you that He can't see from His position. Oh, the comfort, peace, and relief this knowledge should bring to our souls! Seeing Him in action is thrilling. Watching Him come to our aid is breathtaking. Yes, we can see Him fight the battles of life right before our eyes. Not necessarily through physical warfare, but with spiritual sovereignty. Because He sees all, He can act on our behalf before we ever get to where we are going to face what we will be facing. Mind-blowing, I know!

✝ *There isn't anything going on with you that He can't see.*

We can also see many examples of our Mighty God fighting for His people throughout Scripture. In a pep talk to Joshua, the newly appointed leader of the Israelites, Moses said, "Do not be afraid or discouraged, for the LORD will personally go ahead of you. He will be with you; he will never fail you nor abandon you" (Deut. 31:8). And King David, a man after God's own heart (Acts 13:22), who experienced firsthand God's mighty defense, penned this beautiful illustration of God's love and coverage of care. You must read it out loud. Oh, how I wish I could be there to hear you read about how much He loves you!

> You go before me and follow me.
> You place your hand of blessing on my head.
> Such knowledge is too wonderful for me,
> too great for me to understand!

> I can never escape from your Spirit!
>> I can never get away from your presence!
> If I go up to heaven, you are there;
>> if I go down to the grave, you are there.
> If I ride the wings of the morning,
>> if I dwell by the farthest oceans,
> even there your hand will guide me,
>> and your strength will support me.
> I could ask the darkness to hide me
>> and the light around me to become night—
>> but even in darkness I cannot hide from you.
> To you the night shines as bright as day.
>> Darkness and light are the same to you.
>> (Ps. 139:5–12)

The Defender of Every Detail

My friend stood in a deli awestruck and speechless at the work of her Mighty One fighting for her. She experienced firsthand the meaning of "You go before me and follow me. You place Your hand of blessing on my head" and "I can never get away from Your presence!" You see, God's defense is spiritual and physical, and it reaches across time, space, and economics, as well as the mistakes and mishaps of others—even if it involves hoagie sandwiches.

Let me explain. Linda was responsible for planning the year-end celebration of the women's mentoring group at church. Running on little sleep and competing with the hurriedness of the holidays, she decided to keep the preparations as simple as possible: she would order sandwiches, chips, fruit, and water from a local deli. And since the event fell on the same day as her daughter's music therapy, she preordered everything. In her pre-planning, she made sure all the orders were marked with the correct time and date for pickup.

Much to her surprise, her daughter's bus arrived early that day from school; therefore, Linda could take her to music therapy early. This small victory afforded her the luxury of time, which is always helpful, but on this day it would be needed more than usual, though Linda didn't know that yet. However, noticing the generous gift of time, Linda knew God was up to something. He was fighting her battle before she realized she had one.

After therapy, she dropped her daughter off at home, then went to pick up the food order, praising God for the extra time. (Let's face it—ten minutes equals an hour in the schedule of a busy woman.) Joyfully, she strolled in to get her food, only to discover that her order had been marked with the *wrong* pickup date and was not ready at all!

Normally, this news might have flustered and frustrated Linda. But she had complete peace as she rattled off the order for the second time to the young girl behind the counter.

God had given Linda extra time. He defeated *her* battle, an unprepared food order, with time to wait on a new order, and He filled her with His peace so she could display Jesus to everyone at the counter. And there was even icing on the cake (or extra sauce on the hoagie)—there was no charge! Instead, she got a $50 refund and the glory of a testimony to tell her women's group about God's movement in her life.

Our Mighty God has a seat with a view, and oh, the sights He sees. We can't begin to fathom all He accomplishes on our behalf, even down to the smallest details. There is so much defending and weapon wielding that we don't see, because it takes place somewhere our position doesn't allow us—the heavenlies.

We can hop over to the book of Daniel to see a perfect example of this truth. Daniel had prayed about something and had not received an answer. (We've been there, brother Daniel.)

Then [the messenger from God] said, "Don't be afraid, Daniel. Since the first day you began to pray for understanding and to humble yourself before your God, your request has been heard in heaven. I have come in answer to your prayer. But for twenty-one days the spirit prince of the kingdom of Persia blocked my way. Then Michael, one of the archangels, came to help me, and I left him there with the spirit prince of the kingdom of Persia." (Dan. 10:12–13)

For twenty-one days, a battle was fought on Daniel's behalf without his knowledge. Have you ever wondered, *What has God protected me from? Who has He taken down on my behalf? How has He redirected me to a better way?* Friends, it's true, the battle between life and death has been won, but there are little wars going on concerning us that we know nothing about, and probably never will, because our Mighty God is on patrol. Like the watchman who sits in the tower to guard the city, so our God watches and guards His children. God faithfully stays at His post, but do we? What exactly is our position in the battle?

Defense-Ready: Our Position

I'll be the first to admit that I don't know much about sports. When I was younger, I played softball. The ball was pitched. The ball was hit. The batter ran. The game really isn't that complicated. I realize there is coaching involved and strategies to plan, but for the not-so-serious player like me, the basics were simple. Since I have very little knowledge of the big sports, including basketball and football, I will tread lightly and try not to get in over my head.

Most sports teams have two parts: defense and offense. The job of the defense is to stand against the opponent and prevent them from scoring. The offensive team has the role of scoring. The team needs an experienced coach, as well as offensive and defensive players positioned and prepared to play. Every player has a role, and the team depends on the dedication of each player. Not to trivialize life, but the game analogy works, even if you aren't a sports enthusiast.

Like in competitive sports, the kingdom of God needs dedicated team members, positioned and prepared for the game. When we surrender our lives to Jesus Christ, we join Team God. We have an experienced Coach to lead us, both offensively and defensively. He graciously gave us His Word as our playbook, to know how to equip ourselves for victory in life.

† *The kingdom of God needs
dedicated team members, positioned
and prepared for the game.*

In writing this section I've been gripped by a question. As your friend, I sense a responsibility to discuss it with you. The Spirit has taught us beautifully of the might of God. We've learned that He is our Defender, ready to take anyone to the mat, on any plain. He loves us and never allows us to escape His field of vision. These truths are almost too much to take in, wouldn't you say?

However, one thing puzzles me: *If God is my Defender, then why do I need to be positioned and prepared for battle?* Oh, friend, does God have a word for us! Hang on and get ready. We are going to hang out with Daniel for a little longer, then we will visit with Paul in prison as he writes to the church of Ephesus.

God has His position and we have a position too. Daniel demonstrates our battle position. You are going to need your pen or highlighter again as we revisit Daniel 10:12. Highlight two phrases: *pray for understanding* and *humble yourself before your God*.

> Then he said, "Don't be afraid, Daniel. Since the first day you began to *pray for understanding* and to *humble yourself before your God*, your request has been heard in heaven. I have come in answer to your prayer."

Daniel gives us two clear instructions about our battle position. Let's unpack *pray for understanding* first. This phrase indicates that Daniel didn't understand everything that was happening to him. I know you can relate. You read your Bible, pray, worship, go to church, and serve. You know, you do all the right things, yet shrapnel from the warring armies lies at your feet, the attacks linger, and casualties continue. What's a daughter of the Mighty

God to do? She sets her mind to gain understanding by going to the One who understands.

Daniel was a man who made regular visits with God a priority. In fact, he prayed three times a day (Dan. 6:10). In this particular instance, Daniel took praying for understanding to a greater intensity by fasting (10:3). When we seek God with all our hearts, we will find Him (Jer. 29:13). The Scriptures are full of individuals who inquired of the Lord. Rebekah asked the Lord about the wrestling babies in her belly (Gen. 25:22–23), David sought military counsel (1 Sam. 23:2), and the disciples needed assistance in replacing Judas (Acts 1:24–26). Solomon, the wisest king to rule Israel, spoke of gaining understanding:

> Let the wise listen to these proverbs and become
>   even wiser.
> Let those with understanding receive
>   guidance. (Prov. 1:5)

> For the LORD grants wisdom!
> From his mouth come knowledge and
>   understanding. (2:6)

The second positional phrase, *humble yourself before your God*, is easy, if you master the first one. Once again, we can thank Daniel for being a living example of warring rightly—he continually submitted before God, even when he knew his life was on the line, and despite having a high position of earthly authority as adviser to a king. Asking for help is a sign of humility. A know-it-all will not advance very far in understanding. Pride caused Satan to be cast out of heaven; we can't allow it to be the reason God refuses to give us instruction. "Pride ends in humiliation, while humility brings honor" (Prov. 29:23). "So humble yourselves under the mighty power of God, and at the right time he will lift you up in honor" (1 Pet. 5:6).

Standing Firm: Our Preparation and Protection

The apostle Paul was another person who understood the right position to take before our Mighty God in order to follow Him into battle. Though Paul's pride at one point in his life had brought him low, even down to the ground (Acts 9), his experience of the Lord taught him much about gaining understanding and maintaining humility. Thankfully, Paul left behind many of his letters that give us insight into what he learned as he kept walking with God. Let's read some of Paul's mail. He has a lot to teach us about being prepared. You'll need your highlighter again as we look at his letter to the believers at the church of Ephesus:

> A final word: Be strong in the Lord and in his mighty power. Put on all of God's armor so that you will be able to stand firm against all strategies of the devil. For we are not fighting against flesh-and-blood enemies, but against evil rulers and authorities of the unseen world, against mighty powers in this dark world, and against evil spirits in the heavenly places.
>
> Therefore, put on every piece of God's armor so you will be able to resist the enemy in the time of evil. Then after the battle you will still be standing firm. Stand your

ground, putting on the belt of truth and the body armor of God's righteousness. For shoes, put on the peace that comes from the Good News so that you will be fully prepared. In addition to all of these, hold up the shield of faith to stop the fiery arrows of the devil. Put on salvation as your helmet, and take the sword of the Spirit, which is the word of God. (Eph. 6:10–17)

I'm all aboard and stoked about what we've learned about our Mighty God, but as I mentioned earlier, something has gripped me and won't let go. It's a real head scratcher. I wonder, are you wondering too? If God is our Mighty God, ready to take down anyone or anything that seeks to take us down, and if we've been taught our position on His team, then why are we given instructions about putting on the full armor of God? Why do I have to dress for battle if God is the one fighting?

Grab your highlighter and get ready to say "Wowzers!" I wish I could be there with you and we could say it together. Please read the Ephesians passage again. Highlight or underline the words *stand* and *standing.*

Three times Paul tells us we should be standing firm or to stand our ground. (Did you go back and reread the passage?) He does not tell us to advance, attack, shoot, or fire. Our Mighty God is the one leading the offense. We are on the defense. And what are we defending? Our ground—our position as members of Team God.

Paul talks about the spiritual wrestling match taking place in the heavenlies. And what is happening in the spiritual realm is much greater than anything happening here on earth. But the struggles in the physical world, the struggles with flesh-and-blood annoyances—the grouchy coworker, the rebellious child, the inattentive husband, or the slow driver in the passing lane—are often what test the Jesus in us. These all may be part of the "strategies of the devil" to weaken us—to make us stumble and lose our firm footing in our faith.

Life is troublesome and painful. I get it; trust me, I do. Troubles, hurts, heartaches, disappointments, disease, and cruelty come at us. Life is bothersome, painful, and apart from the power of God, impossible to navigate. However, "I consider that our present sufferings are not worth comparing with the glory that will be revealed in us" (Rom. 8:18 NIV).

We've got to grasp this truth: what gets to us is nothing compared to what is going on above us. It's through life's aggravations that we get to know Jesus Everlasting as our Mighty God. Every annoyance gives us the opportunity to humble ourselves and trust Him more. With greater trust comes greater understanding, greater faith, and a closer resemblance to the heavenly Father whose image we want to bear. Any war has casualties and injuries, but God inspired Paul to tell us how to minimize the effect the heavenly war might have on our hearts. Until Christ returns and puts a final end to the battle, we have to follow His instructions: stand firm.

† *What gets to us is nothing compared to what is going on above us.*

After taking our correct position, we prepare ourselves with the correct protection. A football player can't take the field without the proper equipment, nor can we stand grounded firmly in our faith without the correct gear. Let's take a look at each piece of God's armor.

Belt of truth: A belt is the accessory that pulls an outfit together. God's Word is the Christian's source of truth—the standard by which everything else must be measured. The devil is a liar, and his lies are all the more powerful because he knows the truth. Remember? He was an angel. He knows how to twist the truth to trick us. But if he knows the truth, shouldn't we know it even better? If we put on that belt every day—reading God's Word and wrapping our minds in His truth—we will be able to see right through the enemy's deception.

Body armor of righteousness: Body armor, or what in some translations is referred to as the breastplate, protects the heart, the dwelling place of God. It's His righteousness that covers us. Satan will try to call into question our faith with accusations of our past. Jesus covered our past, present, and future with life. We stand firm in the everlasting righteousness that He gave us and that we did nothing to earn.

Shoes of peace: Shoes are the perfect accessories for standing firm, especially a soldier's shoes. The enemy studies our behaviors and knows what buttons to press to steal our peace. But our battle shoes are spiked to ensure our stability. They are reinforced with the knowledge of the gospel—the good news that never gets any less good, no matter how bad of a day we are having. Regardless of what is happening around us, we can always be assured that Jesus died for us and rose again and is now seated at the right hand of God—our everlasting Savior, Redeemer, and Friend.

Shield of faith: Faith is the bedrock of our lives. Naturally, Satan will stir up trouble around us to cause us to doubt what we believe. With our shields of faith, we can repel questioning arrows. Knowing the truth secures our faith and snuffs out the devil's attempts to fan flames of doubt and division in our minds.

Helmet of salvation: Some girls can do the hat thing, but not me; I never could. However, the helmet of salvation is one hat that I wear proudly. Satan's lies and half-truths can't steal my salvation or make me doubt who I am in Christ. Since I have accepted Jesus as my Savior and received His forgiveness, my position is secure. No one can take that away. So go ahead and buckle that chinstrap, friends, because the enemy will target our thoughts to undermine our security.

Sword of the Spirit: We get to boss Satan, because we know God's Word. The soldier's sword of biblical times wasn't long and narrow; it was a small weapon used for close hand-to-hand combat. As Tony Evans put it, "[The devil] is allergic to the Word of God when it is consistently used against him."[2] Even when he comes close to us, we can pull out our Bibles and read verses that will give us strength. And we can memorize verses that provide hope and encouragement, so that we won't lose heart whenever we are in the middle of life's struggles.

Our position, preparedness, and protection are the secrets to minimal casualties. God's got this. All we have to do is stand firm.

In just a minute, we're going to meet a person who was left out in the open—unprotected and unprepared—in the middle of a struggle she couldn't see. She had no firm ground to stand on and wasn't even in the position to be able to stand up for herself. So what happened? Let's keep reading together and find out.

The Woman Caught

"Don't air out your dirty laundry for the world to see." It's one of those longtime popular sayings that means don't put out in public what should remain in private. This could mean anything from hanging your pretty private things on the clothesline (Do those still exist? Clotheslines, I mean, not pretty private things) to airing your family grievances in the middle of a restaurant on a Friday night. "Dirty laundry" could also be a term for sin. Most of us like to keep our sins hidden away from the public eye, just like we keep our delicate dainties hidden in a drawer.

In a few short verses of John 8, we meet another woman whose name we don't know, like the Samaritan woman, but whose sin was left hanging out for all of us to see through the ages. Some men sought to use her to take Jesus down, but as she stood defenseless, our Mighty God took her accusers down without ever throwing a punch. She was publicly shamed and publicly saved in the space of a few paragraphs.

It was an early morning, and Jesus was in Jerusalem for the Feast of Tabernacles, a festival that remembered and celebrated God's provision and protection for His people as they wandered in the desert after the exodus from Egypt. Jesus was in the temple, preaching to a crowd. Then His teachings came to a screeching halt when religious leaders shoved a woman into the middle of His sermon. How is that for a sermon illustration!

> As he was speaking, the teachers of religious law and the Pharisees brought a woman who had been caught in the act of adultery. They put her in front of the crowd. (John 8:3)

The Pharisees were a pious group of middle-class businessmen, which I like to refer to as the self-appointed Torah Police (the Torah is the name given to the first five books of the Bible, also known as the Pentateuch). They were committed to keeping every law of God found in those books and took it upon themselves to be judge and jury in their communities. To them, Jesus was a threat to their leadership but also a threat to their interpretation of the law, so they were constantly trying to find reasons to discredit Him. On this particular day, their plan involved a woman—not an innocent bystander, mind you, but an unwilling participant for sure.

Let's notice they brought her by force, after catching her in the act of sin. Being caught in an intimate moment with a man who was not your husband (but somebody else's) was the very definition of adultery and punishable by public stoning. The plan of the religious police was to finally have a reason to arrest Jesus 'or, at the very least, to make Him look bad in front of His listeners. In their minds, He would either agree to (and perhaps be forced to be involved in) capital punishment, which would not look good for Him publicly, or He would let her go unpunished, standing in direct opposition of the law (vv. 4–6). And if they had to sacrifice a woman to accomplish either of these goals, then so be it. In any case, it would be a win for the leaders.

Something the Pharisees didn't factor in their plan? Jesus always stands by those who are powerless. And He always wins.

Jesus didn't fall for their plan as the accusations were hurled at the woman. Just as the Pharisees had caught the woman by surprise, Jesus's response caught them off guard. Instead of standing up to their legal rhetoric, Jesus stooped down and wrote in the dirt.

> They were trying to trap him into saying something they
> could use against him, but Jesus stooped down and wrote
> in the dust with his finger. (v. 6)

What Jesus wrote isn't known, and I'm not even sure that it really matters. Maybe He was trying to dial down the situation by doodling. Perhaps He was generating a to-do list. Whatever it was, the heat of the moment cooled down. But the men kept pushing for an answer about whether she should be stoned or not, so Jesus had to say something. Now, Jesus has a way with one-liners and pointed questions (maybe it's the counselor in Him), but His words here had to hit like ice water on an open flame.

> They kept demanding an answer, so he stood up again
> and said, "All right, but let the one who has never sinned
> throw the first stone!" (v. 7)

After His statement, He bent down and continued His writing. The elite, who were so full of wisdom and knowledge, were left without words. In fact, they were so convicted that one by one they dropped their stones and walked away. Just the woman stood there still, convicted and caught in sin, but freed from her accusers.

> Then Jesus stood up again and said to the woman, "Where
> are your accusers? Didn't even one of them condemn you?"
>   "No, Lord," she said.

And Jesus said, "Neither do I. Go and sin no more."
(vv. 10–11)

Not a stone was thrown, nor a sword drawn. It was over. A life defended. The woman, perhaps half-clothed and dusty from the aggressive manner in which she was manhandled, walked away. Unscathed from the battle. No open wounds, only a heart forgiven, and brokenness made beautiful.

We don't wake up in the morning expecting to face trouble, but there's a very strong possibility we will. Standing firm in our position, prepared and protected by our Mighty God is the only way to face the day. This woman didn't wake up that morning anticipating public shame on the temple steps, but her Mighty God met her on the battlefield. She didn't choose to be a pawn in a scramble for power, but the Strong One gave her strength to find her feet. She didn't ask to be dragged through the city like a worthless rag, but her Defender made sure she knew she was valued. And perhaps most importantly, she didn't know that day that she would need saving, but our Redeemer set her free. He stood with her and stayed with her, even though the world seemed against her.

He will do the same for us.

Everlasting Thoughts

Remember, don't erase, edit, or omit. Just put pen or pencil to paper and listen to what God is trying to teach you through His Word right now.

Have you ever been in a situation in which you felt defenseless? Write down some of the feelings you had at the time.

Think about a battle you feel you are struggling with right now—it might be a physical battle with illness or a mental battle with a stressful situation or an emotional battle to get your feelings under control. Describe your battle. Now take a step back—for real. Lean back away from your paper, squint a bit, and think about perspective. Circle the different sides in your battle. Who are the primary players? Then consider this—where is God in your battle?

Go back to the verses from Ephesians 6:10–17. Which part of the armor described there stands out to you? How do you feel about your readiness to stand firm in God's protection?

Think about the story of the woman caught in adultery. Write out a description of the battle she got pulled into. Who were the primary characters in that battle? What do you think it looked like from God's perspective?

Clearly, the woman caught in adultery was in the wrong. Yet Jesus acted as her Defender. How would you explain this surprising response to a person who doesn't know much about Jesus?

In what ways do you rely on Jesus to be your Defender? In what ways do you need to trust Him more?

Leaning on the Music: "A Mighty Fortress Is Our God"

Words and music by Martin Luther, 1529

Lean in so I can tell you a secret: I wasn't happy when someone called hymn number 40 on Hymn Night. The reason is silly now, but I'll tell you anyway. This *is* still a judgment-free zone, right? It was the words. The words are the reason I didn't like the song.

Words like *fortress*, *bulwark*, and *amid* were foreign to me. Phrases like *mortal ills prevailing*, *ancient foe*, and *doth seek to work his woe*—what do they mean? Here's the first verse, in case you aren't familiar with the song.

> A mighty fortress is our God,
> A bulwark never failing:
> Our helper He, amid the flood
> Of mortal ills prevailing.
> For still our ancient foe
> Doth seek to work us woe;
> His craft and power are great,

And armed with cruel hate,
On earth is not his equal.

So we're all in agreement, right? These words and phrases aren't exactly easy to work into our twenty-first-century conversation. However, we can't deny that the power and might behind the message of the song are timeless. In a modern-day paraphrase, I believe Luther was trying to say, "God's got this. Everything's gonna be okay."

Confident faith. It's knowing that God is in control, even when things seem out of control. It's believing you are ultimately victorious, even when you experience loss. This kind of faith helps you to stand sure-footed like Moses, waiting for your Red Sea to part (Ex. 14:21), or like Gideon, when your personal armory seems small (Judg. 7).

Time in God's Word and obedience to it build our spiritual confidence. We learn that we can stand firm and stare the enemy right in the face and say, "Nope. Not today. God, the leader of heaven's army, is on my side, and today you lose." We develop an assurance that even though this world is filled with evil, as Martin Luther's words proclaim, the "right Man" is on our side, "the Man of God's own choosing." That Man is Christ Jesus: "From age to age the same / And He must win the battle."

He has power, majesty, and authority to accomplish everything for everyone at any time. He sits on His throne and oversees what is happening everywhere all at once. He walks in the high places:

For the LORD is the one who shaped the mountains,
stirs up the winds, and reveals his thoughts to
mankind.

> He turns the light of dawn into darkness
> and treads on the heights of the earth.
> The LORD God of Heaven's Armies is his
> name! (Amos 4:13)

Though the church I attend, like many, has replaced hymnals with a big screen, every now and again the prelude of this mighty anthem fills the sanctuary. The people in the pews stand tall, at attention. Yes, even me, the one who didn't like hymn 40 (and I'm still not sure what a *bulwark* is). I stand up and belt out the words:

> A mighty fortress is our God,
> A bulwark never failing:
> Our helper He, amid the flood
> Of mortal ills prevailing.

On the other side of many victories, I know without a shadow of a doubt that Jesus is on my side. Even if I occasionally experience defeat, I am ultimately a winner. There isn't anything going on that He can't see from His position in heaven. The woman caught in adultery was not out of His frame of vision and neither are you. Our Mighty God has a seat with a view, and oh, the sights He sees. We aren't privy to the battle He's watching, but we can trust that He's wielding His weapons and dispensing His armies on behalf of His children. He is our Mighty God and our mighty fortress; He will win the battle.

Chapter 4

A Father Who Calls to Us

If you have read any of my previous books or seen me speaking online, you know that I grew up in a home that was very similar to the homes of Wally and Beaver Cleaver (*Leave It to Beaver*) and Bud, Betty, and Kathy Anderson (*Father Knows Best*). If you haven't seen either of those shows, you can probably dig up a clip on YouTube. Just think all-American, wholesome, hardworking, and fully functional. Like those TV moms, June and Margaret, my momma put her career on hold to be with my brother and me, while my daddy went out every day to do his carpentry work. We did life on a cul-de-sac in an 1,800-square-foot brick ranch home that my father had built. We drove around town in our "Woodchuck" (so nicknamed for its laminated wood panels), the Country Squire station wagon, as my parents shuttled us to ball games, ballet class, piano lessons, swim club, and of course, church.

We were members of the large church in the community. You know the one on the corner at the main intersection of town with a chapel as well as a main sanctuary? It had a covered-drive drop-off area so you didn't get your church clothes wet when it rained, a gym for inside recreational activities, and ball fields for outside sports. I'm almost positive you had one just like it in your town; maybe you were even a member.

My parents served in the church: they were on committees, sang in the choir, taught Sunday school, and participated in missions. Dad was on the deacon rotation: on three years, off three years. When the doors were open, we were there … arriving in the Woodchuck. We were there for children's choir, puppet practice, Girls in Action, Royal Ambassadors, and Training Union (like discipleship classes now). We were regulars at every church event: Covered-Dish Dinner-on-the-Grounds, Summer Sunday Night Homemade Ice Cream Socials, sports of various sorts, homecoming, and who can forget, Clean-the-Grounds Day.

My parents didn't just take us to church to learn about Jesus; they demonstrated lives that were all about Jesus and His kingdom. To say I was blessed is an enormous understatement. With examples like these, what little girl wouldn't want to follow Jesus? When I was seven, Jesus came to live in my heart. Seven: before life's temptations could overtake me, evil could get a grip, and my soul was lured away by the tempting pull of sinful living, I chose to follow Jesus.

You might be thinking, *Well, bully for you! My parents divorced when I was three. I never knew my father. My parents didn't even want me, and they let me know it. It must be nice for everything to have been perfect for you.*

I can see how you would think that; really, I do. In fact, I would probably say the same thing about me. And as I said, I understand and value the positive influence my family life had on me. I also understand and have so much compassion for anyone who had a difficult childhood. But what looks perfect from the outside isn't always perfect on the inside. Satan could not steal my salvation, but he sure tried his best to destroy the belief that I was holy and dearly loved (Col. 3:12). For most of my life, Satan, the author of doubt and lies, would have me believe that because of my Norman Rockwell upbringing, I didn't have a testimony—a real story to tell about how Jesus saved me. But the truth is, everyone who has been saved has a testimony.

The Testimony I Always Wanted

My whole life, since I was old enough to sit in big church, I wanted a testimony. I couldn't understand why I didn't have one.

Every so often we'd have a guest speaker come to our church. Our pastor would share the pulpit with one of those people … a person with a testimony. These men and women didn't necessarily have money or position. Some were dressed in fine clothes, while others dressed more casually. I remember some were musical and shared their testimonies through songs. Some "testimony people" had written books. After these authors spoke, the congregation crowded around the book table like we were meeting a celebrity. They didn't look or sound alike, but their messages were similar: *I was a mess. God found me in the pit of despair, cleaned me up, and saved me.* Have you seen or heard any testimony people?

Younger me called them "testimony people." I didn't know what else to call them and honestly was too embarrassed to ask. *Shouldn't a girl who loves Jesus and is at church every time the doors open know what "these" people are called?* I was afraid to ask someone. What if

I was supposed to know and had somehow missed this information because I had forgotten to read my Sunday school lesson? I couldn't risk it. I just remember being intrigued and deeply moved by their stories. Each one emotionally shared how God had rescued them from drug addiction, alcoholism, abusive relationships, or criminal behavior. Some had even been in prison. And for a girl who grew up in a Norman Rockwell painting, this was fascinating.

Their lives were like the before-and-after pictures from any one of those thousand or so makeover shows that are out there now. In the before footage, the person is often not smiling and looks dull and frumpy. In the after picture, they are wearing bright colors and showing a brilliant, freshly bleached grin as big as the state of Texas. And the worse the "before" looks, the more dramatic and exciting the "after" is, right?

I wanted a testimony. I wanted a dramatic story of exciting change, of how God had called me out of my pit of despair and into His service. But my story was simple. I grew up in church, in a Christian home with both parents. They taught me about Jesus and took me to church, and I asked Jesus to live in my heart. Period. The end. No drugs. No abuse. No outlandish living. No criminal life.

Older (and hopefully wiser) Wendy now understands the huge fallacy in thinking that I didn't have a testimony to share just because my life was fairly drama-free. Everyone who wasn't saved and then became saved has a testimony, even someone who was seven when she made the decision to follow Christ. Everyone has a story to share. And all of our stories can be used to share Jesus.

As we turn to study the life of another woman Jesus saved, we'll discover another truth about this misunderstood word, *testimony*.

our testimony doesn't begin and end with our salvation experience. If you write in your books, you might want to highlight or underline that sentence. Salvation is where each of our testimonies starts, and in all honesty, it never ends. It never ends, because our Everlasting Father keeps calling to us, and we have an eternity to have experiences with Him.

> ✝ *Our testimony doesn't begin and end with our salvation experience.*

Every experience we have with God is a testimony. Each time we witness His faithfulness in our lives and His activity in our midst, we have a testimony to tell. Maybe you can take a few minutes to trace the evidence of His faithfulness in your life. Some call these experiences "God winks." Was there a time when your account was empty but you gave anyway? Then, a few days later, an unexpected refund came in the mail for the exact amount of the check you wrote? Was there a time when you prayed for a redeemed relationship? And now, to your surprise, through counseling and the work of the Holy Spirit, you've celebrated another anniversary? Did you walk into the chemo room stricken with fear only to be greeted by Carmen, the nurse with the Jesus smile? And as she inserted the IV, she whispered a prayer over you? Did your husband lose his job when your daughter's college tuition was due? But later you discovered she qualified for grants that did not have to be paid back and those grants covered the entire semester?

YES!!! Those are testimonies. We are testimony people! Declare them right now, as the psalmist did!

> I will tell everyone about your righteousness.
>> All day long I will proclaim your saving
>>> power,
>> though I am not skilled with words.
> I will praise your mighty deeds, O Sovereign
>> LORD.
>> I will tell everyone that you alone are just.
>
> O God, you have taught me from my earliest
>> childhood,
>> and I constantly tell others about the
>>> wonderful things you do.
> Now that I am old and gray,
>> do not abandon me, O God.
> Let me proclaim your power to this new
>> generation,
>> your mighty miracles to all who come after
>>> me. (Ps. 71:15–18)

Oh! Did you notice the psalmist's words "*your* righteousness" and "*your* mighty deeds"? Testimony people don't say "Hey, look at me. Look what I did." Testimony people brag on God. God pulled them from the pit of despair. The Lord was the lifter of their heads and their deliverance. A person with a testimony never forgets the Source of that testimony. The woman we are about to meet never forgot the Source of her deliverance and never stopped following Him. He is the Everlasting Father, who surrendered His life so she could have everlasting with Him.

Mary, the Testimony Woman

In our previous chapters we studied two unnamed women Jesus saved. The woman at the well ran to her town telling all about Jesus's righteous acts and wonderful deeds. The woman who was caught in sin stood in grace as Jesus freed her from condemnation and forgave her. I love that Jesus, in a time when women were given no respect and little value, found women worthy to touch, teach, spend time with, and save! One woman was from Samaria, one He met in Jerusalem, and Mary was met on His second trip through the region of Galilee.

Magdala was a first-century port town on the western shore of the Sea of Galilee, and it was a center for trade and exported salted fish. It is believed that Mary's hometown was Magdala, and therefore to differentiate her from the other Marys in the Bible, she is known as Mary Magdala, or maybe you've seen her referred to as Mary Magdalene.

Like the other women we have met in our encounters, very little is known about this Mary. She is mentioned twelve times in the four Gospels, the biblical narrative of the life of Jesus. Even the details of her life-changing encounter with Jesus are not described in chapter and verse. The sum of her salvation gets but a brief note:

> Soon afterward Jesus began a tour of the nearby towns
> and villages, preaching and announcing the Good News
> about the Kingdom of God. He took his twelve disciples
> with him, along with some women who had been cured
> of evil spirits and diseases. Among them were Mary
> Magdalene, from whom he had cast out seven demons.
> (Luke 8:1–2)

Yes, you read that correctly. Jesus called seven demons out of Mary. Seven is a number often used in the Bible to suggest "completeness." This could mean that the demons had overtaken Mary completely or that the releasing of them resulted in Mary's complete restoration. Either way, I think it's important to park here for a skinny minute and talk about this situation.

What rushes through your mind when you hear the words *demon possessed?* Pitchforks? Long skinny tails? Flames? Hell? Erratic convulsing body movements? Split personalities? Fear? For me, it's all of the above, as well as other unsettling thoughts that I'm unable to put into words. I think of a scary situation, and yet it's heartbreaking at the same time.

Demons and demonic activity are part of the narrative of Scripture. Demons are portrayed in the Bible as spirits and do not have human bodies (Matt. 8:16). Demons are also talked about as being under Satan's control (Matt. 12:24). Demons apparently can think and talk and move (Mark 1:24; Matt. 12:44–45). In Scripture it's not always clear if demon possession was the cause of mental or physical illness, but in Matthew 4:24, for example, the case of demon possession seems to be distinguished from other ailments.

Without going into a full course on demonology (because that sounds awful), we can safely say that according to Scripture, demons are very real and they do affect people in an assortment of horrible ways. Satan, under God's sovereignty, rules the world right now: "We know that we are children of God and that the world around us is under the control of the evil one" (1 John 5:19). He and those who were thrown out of heaven with him have permission to mess with, manipulate, and meander around the world, influencing circumstances to stunt the growth of believers' faith and destroy their testimonies. This is why everything we learned in chapter 3 is so important: we must be prepared to stand firm in our faith.

The Life That Mary Lived

We have no specific information about the demons that possessed Mary, how often they reared their ugliness, or how long she endured them. Nor does Scripture explain why demons were permitted to enter people at all. Some experts have speculated God allowed this so that Jesus's authority could be demonstrated.

But we do know that Mary Magdalene was one of many individuals who suffered from the mental and physical torment brought about by demons. This must have been a terribly frightening way to live. People in the Bible who had demons were isolated and shunned. They were kept away from others because their problem was not well understood and their actions were unpredictable.

Oh, how Mary needed Jesus!

But after the demons were cast out, she appeared to bounce back, and she dedicated her life to the Lord. Let's go back to the mention of Mary from Luke 8, when Jesus was touring towns and preaching the good news. He took His disciples along with Him, as well as women He had cured.

> Among them were Mary Magdalene, from whom he had cast out seven demons; Joanna, the wife of Chuza, Herod's business manager; Susanna; and many others who were contributing from their own resources to support Jesus and his disciples. (vv. 2–3)

Our Mary had money. There isn't information about her entrepreneurial initiatives or business skills. However, we clearly see that she, as well as Joanna and Susanna, could not only afford to travel with Jesus, but they were willing to financially support Him. When the demons left Mary's body, the saving grace of Jesus filled it, and Mary responded to Jesus out of her gratitude.

> † *When the demons left Mary's body, the saving grace of Jesus filled it.*

Her earthly experiences with her Savior, protector, and nurturer, her Everlasting Father, began somewhere along the shoreline of the Sea of Galilee and ended when Jesus ascended to heaven (Mark 16:19). She followed along the dusty roads of His ministry, witnessed the feeding of the five thousand, heard the Sermon on the Mount, saw the healing of the sick and the raising of the dead. Mary stood among the crowd to hear Pontius Pilate sentence her Messiah to death. She kneeled before the cross with His mother as He breathed His last breath. Perhaps her most glorious moment with the Everlasting Father was at the empty tomb, where she was among the first to declare that Jesus is risen. I get excited just typing those words! Don't you love hearing them?!

Whatever her life was like before Jesus didn't matter; she was a new woman. Her life after Jesus was all about Jesus. His life sacrificed for her was worthy of her life surrendered to Him. Certainly, Mary had a testimony.

Mary is proof that you don't have to be a social media sensation, a bestselling author, a podcast phenom, or number one on the Who's Who among Christian Preachers (I just made that up) to make a difference for the kingdom of God. For a woman who is mentioned only twelve times in the Bible, Mary made quite an impact.

On the western slope of the Mount of Olives at the Garden of Gethsemane stands a church topped with seven domes, each boasting a cross. The church celebrates Mary of Magdala and is named for her, St. Mary of Magdala. A saint is a person revered for personal holiness in his or her life. She knew her Everlasting Father; she lived to know Him and make Him known.

Now, I know what you're thinking—Mary's story was one of dramatic change, just like the stories of those testimony people I so admired as a young person in church. I mean, she went from being lost and demon possessed to standing ready to dress the Messiah's body at His tomb. I think she is definitely in the running for the

Most Improved Disciple award. But the thing that Mary helps me to see, and the thing I later realized about my testimony, is that every believer is called to live the life Mary lived after she met Jesus: a life that is surrendered, sanctified, and shared. Don't let those churchy words throw you off the rails—the writer in me just can't resist the alliteration. We'll break down each of these in simple terms, so just hang in there with me.

A Life Surrendered

Christie and I have been friends for fifty years. I've shared the story about how our friendship began in my other books, so I won't repeat the details. To say that we have had many adventures is an understatement. At the age that I am (insert smirk), I don't remember a lot of the little details about our fun and sometimes-crazy antics, but I do remember that I liked to be the one to make decisions.

Generally, every time we had a playdate, or hung out (tweens and teens don't have playdates, right?), I dictated the agenda. I handed out the roles and scripts of what we would do. I was the one in charge. I remember being pretty subtle about it too, easily manipulating the conversation with her (or with any friend for that matter) to play what I wanted to play. Oh, and if I didn't like the rule of some game we were playing, I'd change it. Parker Brothers didn't have anything on me when it came to making rules for board games. Politely stated, I had the gift of persuasion. Bluntly told, I was bossy.

Bossy. In charge. Decision maker. These attributes do not scream life surrendered. In fact, these phrases represent the exact opposite. *Surrender* means "to yield to the power of another." Yep, I'm afraid so.

For those who score high in Administration and Leadership on the spiritual-gifts inventory, whose top strengths in Strength Finders are "Woo" and "Command," and for my fellow 8s on the Enneagram, the concept of *surrender* turns over our apple cart. Surrendering is not part of our natural bent. In the surrendered life, "me and mine" don't work. God is the boss, the Holy Spirit is our guide, and Jesus is our Savior. Period. No further discussion needed.

The idea of surrendering our lives to receive the gift of salvation and eternity with our Everlasting Father sounds inviting. Especially since, as Charles Spurgeon put it, "There is no unfathering Christ, and there is no unchilding us. He is everlastingly a Father to those who trust in Him."[1] We can trust that God, unlike people, will not let us down, but will be with us forever. Sounds pretty terrific, right?

Yes, surrendering to receive sounds just fine—as long as no one tells me what to do.

Oops.

You know, some of my favorite teachers in school (even though they each gave me a C in Conduct—read more about that in chapter 6) were the ones who made me lean in to listen. They used techniques like low tones and long pauses. Jesus also knew how to draw in His audience. He used a well-known teaching method of shuffling around words to create riddle-like statements. In Luke 9:24, He said this: "If you try to hang on to your life, you will lose it. But if you give up your life for my sake, you will save it."

Sentences like these make you stop and think. *How can you save something you give up? How can you lose something by holding on to it?* Let's think this through together.

✝ How *can you save* something *you give up?*

Jesus gave an incredibly bold warning concerning life and death, and the two phrases He used played off each other. If we try to preserve our lives, our earthly lives, by how the world tells us to live, we will most certainly come to eternal death. However, if we lose our lives, if we tell the world "I'm going to live by a standard opposite of what you deem valuable," then we will find life eternal, a life everlasting with Jesus. I outlined this in my book *Yes, No, and Maybe: Living with the God of Immeasurably More.* In saying no to ourselves, we say yes to God and live a life better than the one in our dreams. Jesus made the type of surrender He was talking about even clearer: "If any of you wants to be my follower, you must give up your own way, take up your cross daily, and follow me" (Luke 9:23).

Dying to self in a self-centered world is difficult, unless we remember our Daddy. He died once so that we could live forever. Our forever Father will never leave us or forsake us (Heb. 13:5). Our Father will supply everything we need for all eternity according to His riches in glory (Phil. 4:19). We never have to be concerned about being loved, forgiven, or accepted, because our Daddy is a forever and ever Father. This is the kind of Father a child wants to obey and please. The surrendered life becomes second nature when we keep our eyes on forever with Jesus Everlasting. Forfeiting our wants for His ways will not make sense to the world; however, it will translate to a life full of love, joy, and peace for everyone who follows Him. It's in dying to self that we enjoy real living.

Sweet Mary M. denied herself. She made the decision to carry her cross long before Jesus died on it for her. Wow! Just wow! A life surrendered is a life filled with experiences of Christ—all testimonies to tell.

A Life Sanctified

Sanctified is one of those churchy words that intimidates people, kinda like the King James Version of the Bible, which by the way, I do love. *Sanctified* sounds lofty, pious, and unattainable. It sounds formal, like priestly garments and choir robes—old-school and outdated. Oh, but this old-school girl wishes it were talked about more (and sung from the hymnal every now and then, just saying). *Sanctification*, then, is the process of becoming sanctified, and it distinguishes Christians from the rest of the world.

First, let's talk about what *sanctified* is not. I think that will make everyone feel better. Does that sound okay? Sanctified does not mean you must

- read only the King James Bible;
- wear pantyhose and skirts to church (Where do you even buy pantyhose?);
- fill your music app with only hymns;
- understand everything in the Bible;
- speak Hebrew and Greek;

- know all the books of the Bible, in order; or
- be like Mary Poppins … practically perfect in every way.

Please know I'm not trying to sound irreverent or poke fun at such an important process in the life of a believer. I just feel like I need to lighten the load of such a weighty word. When we have preconceived ideas about certain concepts, we tend to shut down the possibility of learning something new and helpful. Personally, this word has overwhelmed me most of my life—even now, because I know the real me, the parts of me that only God and I know. The secret sin that, even though He said it was forgiven, I still believe can't be redeemed. How can a messed-up sinner like me have any part of such a word like *sanctified*? Have you ever asked yourself a similar question?

Sanctified, in its most simple definition, means "to be set apart" or "to be made holy." Don't let the *h* word make you shrink back like a frightened turtle. By accepting Jesus as our Savior, we are already set apart. But we don't appear different, usually, and unless we give testimony to our salvation, no one really knows it. However, not giving a testimony doesn't make it not so. When Jesus saves your soul, wipes away your sin, and forgives you, you will feel compelled to tell. It's a must-tell situation! You will *not* be able to *not* tell (my apologies again to all the English teachers). You will be like the woman running from the well. Some people tell the world by walking down the aisle of their church. Many choose to outwardly express their new inward reality by participating in baptism.

My point? We don't have to be worried about being holy. We are already holy. We are set apart. You and I have been declared holy, not because of anything we've done, but because of the finished work of the cross. Christ's death covered our sins, and when our Father God sees you, when He sees me, He sees only Jesus. Jesus Everlasting. Doesn't that take your breath away? "For God made Christ, who never sinned, to be the offering for our sin, so that we could be made right with God through Christ" (2 Cor. 5:21).

† *You and I have been
declared holy.*

Glory to God! Such a thought is too much for me to take in, but we do need to move on. So if Jesus's sacrifice made me sanctified, then what do *I* have to do with the process? And how exactly does this connect to Mary Magdalene?

A sanctified life is simply a life living up to its name. Much more than gaining an understanding of the word *sanctified*, my prayer for you is that you will long to live a sanctified life. In other words, a lifestyle that reflects what we are—holy and set apart. We shouldn't do anything that would reflect poorly on our Father. We should instead busy ourselves with actions and behaviors that reflect the freedom and power of a Spirit-led life.

When my children were young but old enough to start having some freedoms, I would frequently say to them, "Remember whose you are." They knew exactly what I meant. As their parents, Scott and I expected them to live up to the godly standard our home represented but, most importantly, to live up to the name of the One who saved them. God has standards and expects His children to follow them, and moreover, when we do follow them, we find the life we've always wanted. A life full of boundless love, limitless grace, and endless mercy … with a Father who is always there to give counsel and defend us.

Mary invested in the sanctification process. Even though her name is only mentioned twelve times, we can be certain she lived a set-apart life—a life that goes against the way the world would have you think and do. Mary put her energy and finances into following Jesus. And her investment paid off.

Her life was made whole by His teachings. Her faith grew and solidified with each miracle she witnessed. Think about it. If none of this were true, then why would she follow Him? Why would she risk her life by being in the crowd when He was convicted, at the cross when He was crucified, and at the tomb ready to anoint His corpse? She had lost her old life and found a better life with Jesus.

We are called to the same life. "You must be holy because I am holy" (1 Pet. 1:16). Mary Magdalene demonstrated the how-tos of holy living:

- Follow Jesus, wherever He directs.
- Listen to what He says: read the Bible and obey it.
- Invest thoughtfully: use your time, talents, and finances to care for others.
- Take risks: leave your comforts, and don't be ashamed to be a follower.

Mary trusted Jesus, and Jesus trusted Mary. It was still dark when Mary arrived at the tomb to pour the burial spices on Jesus. Her heart skipped a beat when she saw the stone that had sealed the tomb had been rolled away. She ran to tell Peter and the others. They all hurried to the tomb, then after confirming Mary's news, Peter and John left. I'm sure Mary thought being saved and delivered from evil was the best moment of her life, but these few moments at the tomb had to rival that. Let's read about this scene from John 20:11–16:

Mary was standing outside the tomb crying, and as she wept, she stooped and looked in. She saw two white-robed angels, one sitting at the head and the other at the foot of the place where the body of Jesus had been lying. "Dear woman, why are you crying?" the angels asked her.

"Because they have taken away my Lord," she replied, "and I don't know where they have put him."

She turned to leave and saw someone standing there. It was Jesus, but she didn't recognize him. "Dear woman, why are you crying?" Jesus asked her. "Who are you looking for?"

She thought he was the gardener. "Sir," she said, "if you have taken him away, tell me where you have put him, and I will go and get him."

"Mary!" Jesus said.

She turned to him and cried out, "Rabboni!" (which is Hebrew for "Teacher").

Jesus called to Mary. He could've spoken to Peter or John. Jesus could've revealed himself to His mother, to ease her suffering. But He chose to speak to Mary first. She was the first person to see and speak to the resurrected Lord! Let that sit with you for a moment. In a day when the words of a woman weren't considered credible, Jesus trusted Mary with the message of His resurrection.

Though a few moments before the day had seemed so dark and Mary might have felt abandoned, with just a word all of that changed. The Everlasting Father, the Lord of her life had never left her, just as He had promised. He had come back to call her by name.

The Everlasting Father calls you by name too. Jesus said, "I am the good shepherd; I know my own sheep, and they know me, just as my Father knows me and I know the Father. So I sacrifice my life for the sheep" (John 10:14–15). He gave His life so you could be called holy. And one day He will come back to claim you as His own face to face.

The sanctified life is not perfect. We're still human. But we are the Everlasting Father's children. And the sanctified life is our way of saying, "Thank You, Daddy. I'll do my best to remember whose I am."

A Life Shared

Sharing is not something that comes naturally to most of us. Spend some time with a couple of toddlers (or teenagers) and you will see what I mean. In fact, shortly after learning to say "Mama" and "Dada," a toddler learns to say "Mine." We learn at an early age this economic lesson: anything worth working for is worth holding on to. You make the money and buy something; it's yours. And the minute we loosen the grip on our goods and decide to share, the valuable item is returned damaged or in poor condition.

When you make minimum wage, there's not a lot of extra. I get it. Sharing is a struggle of mine too. I don't have fine things, and truly I don't have a longing for fine things. Currently, I drive a twelve-year-old car and live in a semi-updated, forty-year-old house. Most of my clothes come from thrift stores. I've seen God work financial miracles my whole life. He is Jehovah-Jireh, "God will provide." And yet, being generous is still hard to do.

Sharing wasn't an issue for Mary. The nosey me wants to know the source of her wealth. Did she sew? Could she have been the personal seamstress for some wealthy women? Maybe she farmed. Did she sell baked goods? Perhaps she owned a food tent close to the port and fed those coming to Magdala for trade and commerce. Oh, there's so much we don't know, but we know what's most important: she was willing to share what she had.

Gratitude generates giving. I'm sure Mary had a very grateful heart. She was free! There were no longer voices in her head or demons in her body. Her soul was now at peace and would be forever, all because of this man named Jesus. Jesus gave, so Mary gave. Her Everlasting Father took care of the needs (material, physical, healing, mental, spiritual) of others, and therefore she imitated Him.

✝ *Gratitude generates giving.*

Giving isn't always about money, another wonderful truth taught in *Yes, No, and Maybe.* Luke 8:3 gives us some insight into what I am talking about. Let's check out the Amplified Version.

And Joanna, the wife of Chuza, Herod's household manager; and Susanna; and many others, who ministered to and provided for Him and them out of their property and personal belongings. (AMPC)

Underline the word *giving*—wait, *giving* isn't in this translation of the verse, but the word *ministered* is. The word for *minister* or *serve* in Greek means "caring for the needs of others as the Lord guides in an active, practical way" or "to provide, take care of, distribute, the things necessary to sustain life."[2] It's very possible that Mary and the other ladies washed out the disciples' tunics and cloaks, as well as shopped for and prepared their food. Basically, these women shared their lives and livelihoods to sustain Jesus and the disciples.

You might not have extra money. But can you help with someone's practical needs? Does your church have a list of people with needs? Do you have a vehicle? Maybe someone needs a ride. What can you do for others that they cannot do for themselves?

Griffin, my twenty-year-old, lives a shared life. If the Holy Spirit prompts him to help, give, or share, he does. Each time he shares his life, he comes home or calls and says, "You're not gonna believe what God did."

A few months back, Griffin was driving down a busy, hilly, four-lane highway. As he came over the top of a hill, he noticed a man in a wheelchair making his way down the road. Eighteen-wheelers and other cars were zooming by, without the courtesy of changing lanes. Griffin drove by the man, and the Spirit told him to turn around. So at the next intersection, Griffin turned around. His heart was beating out of his chest. He had no idea what would happen or how the man would respond, but he knew God.

Griffin soon found out that the man in the wheelchair had lived a rough life and had been in an accident that cost him both legs. Somewhere along in his travels, his prosthetic legs had been stolen. He was getting to where he was going the best way he knew how. Also, he had a few homemade cardboard signs, but they didn't ask for money. His signs were about God's goodness and God's love. Turns out that this man, Alan, was a Christian.

Griffin lifted Alan into the cab of his truck and folded and secured his wheelchair in the bed. The next part of Alan's journey became a little bit lighter because Griffin shared his life with him. Alan got a good night's sleep, a bath, dinner, and some pocket money. Griffin? He got a testimony.

Mine doesn't fit into the vernacular of a shared life. Sharing will always be a struggle for us, unless we remove the word *mine* from our vocabulary. Satan uses that word, as well as the idea of entitlement—that we "deserve" extravagance and more stuff—to keep us from receiving the blessings that come from living the shared life. As Paul said in Acts 20:35, "I have been a constant example of how you can help those in need by working hard. You should remember the words of the Lord Jesus: 'It is more blessed to give than to receive.'"

Let's head back to the Old Testament for one more fundamental message concerning our "stuff." When we live with an attitude of gratitude, remove *mine* from our vocabulary, and internalize the truth of Psalm 24:1, we can begin living the lavishness of a shared life: "The earth is the LORD's, and everything in it. The world and all its people belong to him." What we think we have in our hands isn't even ours. Shocker, right? We just get the blessing of stewarding what we have received.

You may not be called a saint and have a church named after you, but you are no less important to the Everlasting Father. You have a forever Father, one who sits on the throne, who sent His Son so that you will never be separated from Him. You have a Father who always comes back for you, who does care, who is so happy you were born, who has celebrated every accomplishment with you, who has provided for and protected you, and who will dance with you at the wedding celebration in heaven. Oh, dear one, He is your Everlasting Father. He will not change. Follow Him with confident courage.

Everlasting Thoughts

Remember, don't erase, edit, or omit. Just put pen or pencil to paper and listen to what God is trying to teach you through His Word right now.

What words or pictures come to mind when you think of earthly father figures? What would be a good example of a fatherly role model?

What words or pictures come to mind when you think of our
Everlasting Father? How do His characteristics compare to those of
earthly fathers?

Take a moment to write out a brief version of your testimony. When
and how did you get to know Jesus? If you have not accepted Christ
as your personal Savior yet, use this space to write about your experience and thoughts about Christianity.

Now put yourself in the sandals of our Mary M.—Mary of Magdala.
If you had to summarize her testimony, what would you say? Go back
and read the verses about her mentioned in this chapter, if needed.

Read Luke 9:23–25. What does it mean to you to surrender your life for Christ? What part of your life have you not surrendered completely to Him yet?

Read Hebrews 9:11–15, 24–28. Think about the comparison between animal sacrifices made by the Israelites as a part of cleansing ceremonies and the sacrifice made by Jesus Christ. What are the differences? What are the similarities?

Give a definition in your own words of what *sanctify* means as a believer. How are we sanctified?

Read Acts 20:17–38, about Paul saying farewell to the elders of the church at Ephesus. What parts of this passage stand out to you as showing how much Paul had shared his life with these believers? Highlight all the ways you see that sharing occurred, whether in physical or monetary resources, or in other ways.

What would it look like for you to share your life with others as our heavenly Father has shared His life with us?

Leaning on the Music: "Good, Good Father"

Words and music by Pat Barrett
and Tony Brown, 2015

What are the characteristics of a good father? How about a good, good father? It's always fun to conduct a quick web search when such questions pop in our minds. In this case, my search for answers to these questions didn't disappoint; lots of opinions and counsel were waiting for me. My favorite search result was something like "11 Ways to Be a Christian Father (with pictures)." Yes, it said "with pictures." Are you fighting the impulse to run to your computer? Oh, the places Google can take us!

I spent some time reading what godly experts said about being a good Christian father. Words like *loving, involved, nurturing, patient, disciplinarian, attentive*, and *wise* kept appearing. Every page mentioned some variation of these characteristics. After about twenty minutes, though, I stopped clicking because I realized something: even the "good" ones disappoint us, and not one of those earthly fathers is a substitute for our heavenly Father, who is perfect in all of His ways.

He's perfect in love, devotion, involvement, discipline, and patience. God is wise and attentive to every detail of our lives. He is steadfast and true. Our heavenly Father is a promise keeper as well as a dream giver. He is benevolent and kind, always working for our good.

In 2016, I was preparing to walk onto a stage, experiencing the fulfillment of a dream my good, good Father had placed in my heart ten years prior; that's when I first heard "Good, Good Father." Ten years of waiting, questioning, doubt, and tears had led to that moment. A decade of man's rejection of God's plan was now over. There I stood, ready to teach through the lessons of my first book, *Wait and See: Finding Peace in God's Pauses and Plans.* Tears of joy and overwhelming gratitude filled my eyes as I stumbled through the words of this unfamiliar song. Wait? What did it say? "Perfect in all of Your ways"? Oh, yes, yes, He is!

His ways are perfect and undeniable, even though they are so often unexplainable. "'My thoughts are nothing like your thoughts,' says the Lord. 'And my ways are far beyond anything you could imagine. For just as the heavens are higher than the earth, so my ways are higher than your ways and my thoughts higher than your thoughts'" (Isa. 55:8–9). We don't always understand the hardships we have to endure, but neither do we understand the peace He gives us during our suffering or the shocking joy we feel when He calls us, just as He called to Mary in the garden so long ago, and draws us deeper and deeper into His love.

And perhaps the biggest mystery for us is the one that caused tears to fill my eyes as I stood there in the shadows, not feeling at all worthy of the spotlight about to be shone on me. It's that beautiful mystery of how this good and perfect Father can look at me and say He's pleased—pleased by me!—and how I can know that "I'm never alone." How He knows just what I need before I say a word. And how He, over and over again, claims me as His very own, and I know that I'm loved by Him—that's "who I am." I am His loved one. "For God so loved the world that he gave his one and only Son, that whoever believes in him shall not perish but have eternal life" (John 3:16 NIV).

Chapter 5

A Friend Who Brings Us Permanent Peace

Over the river and through the woods to Grandmother's house I'd go. My family would pile into the station wagon and drive out to the country for Sunday lunch at Grandma's.

She'd rise before daylight to sweeten the tea, baste the roast, fry the chicken, season the beans, boil the corn, cream the potatoes, and roll the dough for biscuits. She set out the plates, silverware, and glasses, placed all the homemade desserts on the dining room buffet, and tidied up before leaving for church.

When church was over, there wasn't a lot of socializing, because her family was coming for dinner. She'd exchange pleasantries with the pastor, dash home, strap on her tattered apron, and place the biscuits and cornbread in the oven. What a feast! It wasn't just dinner; it was an event! Even though it was a common occurrence, it was a special occasion. Anytime you dined at Mrs. Nellie's house, it was an event to remember.

She scurried to give us quick side hugs as we came into the house. Steam rose from the stovetop. The corn was boiling, the beans were simmering, and the potatoes were warming. The hum of the exhaust fan muffled all small talk. All movement ceased when the old clock on the mantel struck 12:30. Grandma called us to the kitchen. We'd form a single-file line to fill our plates from her bounty before heading to the dining room, where we'd wait for her to sit down (she was always the last to sit). Then we'd pray. Grandma sat in the chair closest to the kitchen; in case someone forgot something, she could quickly get it.

She served us; she served others. You could fill the ocean with all the cakes and pies she baked for the World Hunger Bazaar at church and the meals she prepared for the shut-in and the sick. Her service was a natural extension of the love she had for her Prince of Peace. She loved Him so! She studied His Word, taught Sunday school, and led circle meeting (known today as small group Bible study) for many years.

She was always busy—teaching, cooking, serving, or tending to her garden—but she was never too busy for her Lord. She never neglected her Lord. Her life was full of situations that would cause the average woman to crumble, but she didn't, because she trusted her Prince to steady her way when times were hard. My grandmother was a harmonious blend of the next two women we are going to meet— sisters who, like Mrs. Nellie, enjoyed having company for dinner.

Guess Who's Coming to Dinner

I LOVE dinner parties! It doesn't matter if I'm eating a burger on Chinet's finest or filet mignon on Royal Patrician china. Whether hosting or attending, dining with friends charges my battery. The room is full of energy, laughter, and storytelling. Hungry bellies and happy faces, oh, it does my heart good! Whether I'm serving dinner for four or forty, I want to have everything in place; serving bowls for each food item, pretty platters filled with pretty food, tablescapes displayed, and candles flickering. The plan is to have everything ready ahead, so when the guests arrive, I can greet them at the door and make them feel special.

Mary and Martha lived in the town of Bethany with their brother Lazarus. The family was well known in their community; in fact, Bethany, located on the eastern slope of the Mount of Olives, was two miles from Jerusalem and is often referred to as the village of Mary and Martha. Scripture doesn't tell us how the three siblings first met Jesus, but we do know that He loved them (John 11:5). Jesus was a repeat guest in their home.

Good friends are priceless, aren't they?

Late one night, a few years ago, my husband and I had an intense moment of fellowship … *real* intense. Maybe you've had some of that kind of fellowship in your marriage and you know what I'm talking about. After slamming a few doors and mumbling to myself, I decided to get in my car to drive it out. I had no idea where I was going; I just drove. Before leaving my neighborhood, I texted my bestie and asked if I could come over. Shattered and worn out from this situation, I needed a safe place to land. She greeted me at the door and sat with me while I cried. Sometimes, you need to be with your friends where you don't have to be fixed up, tidied up, and pulled together. The place of no pretense, where you can show up and recline, relax, and cry if you need to.

Jesus was the same way. It's hard for us to imagine that Jesus the Healer, Son of God, Man of Miracles, and Savior of the World needed friends. But after feeding the five thousand (Luke 9:10–17); experiencing the Transfiguration with Peter, James, and John (Luke 9:28–36); healing a demon-possessed boy (Luke 9:37–43); and facing Samaritan opposition (Luke 9:51–56), Jesus needed time with His friends.

He was downtrodden. He said to His disciples, "Foxes have dens to live in, and birds have nests, but the Son of Man has no place even to lay his head" (Luke 9:58). He knew where He could go to lay His head, relax, and be cared for—the home of Martha. The superb hospitality He found in Martha's home was extremely important to Him. I think Jesus enjoyed Martha's cooking and care. Who doesn't like to be served in that way?

Have you ever had a pop-in visit from a friend? Jesus didn't have access to direct messaging, Snapchat, email, or phones to ask if He could visit. There was no time for Martha to shout to the family, "Guess who's coming to dinner!" Jesus just showed up at Martha's house. She wasn't able to put out fresh towels, light the scented candles, clean off her countertops, or finish folding the laundry. Perhaps breakfast and lunch dishes were still in the sink.

As Jesus and the disciples continued on their way to Jerusalem, they came to a certain village where a woman named Martha welcomed him into her home. (Luke 10:38)

Can you imagine the fire that visit ignited under Martha's feet? Jesus had come to see her family, and she had nothing prepared. I see a little bit of Mrs. Nellie—a shuffle to the door to offer Him a side hug and a quick hello, then off to the kitchen. Water splashing and flames crackling as Martha began to prepare a meal. The exchange of small talk was drowned out with the banging of pots and pans. And I wonder if she murmured under her breath, "Where is that sister of mine?"

> Her sister, Mary, sat at the Lord's feet, listening to what he taught. But Martha was distracted by the big dinner she was preparing. (Luke 10:39–40)

It appears Mary heard all the hustle and bustle, but rather than helping her sister, she sat with Jesus. She sensed no urgency to help prepare a meal. Mary ignored all the background noise from the kitchen and focused her attention on the guest of honor.

Maybe Mary heard Martha's call but decided to listen to Jesus instead. Mary was listening; Martha was doing. If you're like me, the response you've been taught in church is to commend Mary and condemn Martha. But perhaps you are Team Martha and agree Mary was being lazy, as well as disrespectful to her sister. Or you are Team Mary and feel Martha was overreacting and should've been sitting with Jesus too. Before we choose sides, let's see what we can learn about peace from these two sisters, who both loved Jesus.

Martha: The Distracted Sister

Though I have had many sisters in Christ, I don't have a biological sister. Wes is my only sibling. Our parents had us late in life, so it's just the two of us. I remember Wes as the smart one who always got good grades, and he most likely remembers me as the nosey, pesky little sister who followed him around. We really didn't have much of a rivalry, like many brothers and sisters. However, I do recall tattling to my parents when he wasn't doing something he should be doing, or whining because he was given permission to do something that I *didn't* get to do.

Maybe that's how Martha felt. We can assume by her take-charge attitude and owning the house that she was the oldest in the family. It's common for the older child to boss the younger kids and fuss when they seem to be getting away with something. But Martha's frustration was about more than baby sister not helping out in the kitchen—Mary had committed a major cultural faux pas. In this time period, a woman would never be found in the dining area. Only men would recline at the table, discussing current events while women were to be in the kitchen, tending to their domestic duties. (Before we go making protest signs, we have to remember that this was a very different time *and* that Jesus did talk to both Mary and Martha, which shows His love and respect for women.)

I can just imagine the chaotic scene in the kitchen: Martha racing back and forth frantically trying to put together a feast fit for Jesus and several of His friends. While the almonds were roasting and her hands were stuck in the dough, she leaned back from the counter to peek around the corner. The sight she saw set her ablaze: Mary sitting there—just sitting!—hanging on every word Jesus said.

Wiping her floured hands on her apron, Martha marched into the dining area. All the pent-up chatter that had been rattling around in her head finally escaped from her lips. She could not hold her emotions together for one more second.

But Martha was distracted by the big dinner she was preparing. She came to Jesus and said, "Lord, doesn't it seem unfair to you that my sister just sits here while I do all the work? Tell her to come and help me." (Luke 10:40)

Whew! Don't you know that she felt better. Or did she? Sometimes when our thoughts creep out of our mouths, there's instantaneous regret. I wonder if Martha had regret. Her outburst not only publicly maligned her sister for not being where she was supposed to be but called into question Jesus's authority and judgment. Jesus's response to Martha (Luke 10:41) was much kinder than her attitude toward Mary.

But the Lord said to her, "My dear Martha, you are worried and upset over all these details!"

And if I may, please let me include another translation. Oh, how I love God's Word!

"Martha, Martha," the Lord answered, "you are worried and upset about many things." (NIV)

Please underline Martha's name in that last version—yes, both times. I'll be honest, until I studied this text in preparation for writing this manuscript, I read "Martha, Martha" with tones of frustration and strong rebuke. Like when you were young, and your momma called your full name more than once because you were late for dinner or you put the milk carton back in the refrigerator empty. Boy, was I wrong!

When a name is repeated twice in the Bible, the person speaking is preparing the person listening for a great spiritual truth or insight. God called "Abraham! Abraham!" when he was about to sacrifice Isaac (Gen. 22:11). When wrestling with Jacob about a new name, God called "Jacob! Jacob!" (Gen. 46:2). Jesus called "Simon, Simon" (Luke 22:31) when He predicted Peter's denial, and "*Eloi, Eloi*" ("My God, My God") just before He breathed His last (Mark 15:34–38).

"Martha, Martha" was said in tender tones, with gentleness and concern. Oh, don't you know Martha's temperature must have changed quickly. "A gentle answer deflects anger, but harsh words make tempers flare" (Prov. 15:1). Yes, with a calm word, Jesus took control of that conversation. His loving reply softened Martha's heart, readying it for a spiritual truth that is good for all of us to hear.

> But the Lord said to her, "My dear Martha, you are worried and upset over all these details! There is only one thing worth being concerned about. Mary has discovered it, and it will not be taken away from her." (Luke 10:41–42)

Let's clarify a couple of things before we study God's amazing truth for us. Martha wasn't called out because she was preparing a meal for Jesus. Jesus doesn't forbid hospitality. You may recall these words from Hebrews 13:2: "Don't forget to show hospitality to strangers, for some who have done this have entertained angels without realizing it!" And Jesus wasn't just being critical—He loved Mary,

Martha, and Lazarus. So then why did Jesus correct Martha? It wasn't Martha's *actions* that concerned Jesus; it was her *aim*.

> ✝ *Her aim was to create an event, but Jesus wanted her to have an experience.*

Jesus saw Martha's heart. "The LORD doesn't see things the way you see them. People judge by outward appearance, but the LORD looks at the heart" (1 Sam. 16:7). He could see her irritation was a by-product of a distracted heart. "But Martha was distracted by all the preparations that had to be made" (Luke 10:40 NIV). The Greek word for "distracted" is *perispao*. It means "to be drawn away," "to be driven about mentally," or "to be over-occupied, too busy."[1] Like Mrs. Nellie, Martha had many details to oversee in order to prepare the big dinner for an untold number of guests. And let's remember that she didn't have a microwave to warm up anything, nor did she have an Instant Pot to speed up the cooking. All she knew was that many hungry people were in her house and she needed to feed them. But unlike Mrs. Nellie, Martha didn't appear to have come right from spending time worshipping the Lord. Instead, activity and busyness seemed to take priority over spiritual rest. Martha was buried beneath her busy.

Jesus knew all that troubled Martha and wanted to help. Her friend, her Prince of Peace, had arrived at her home, and yet she was too frenzied to receive what He was giving. Her aim was to create an event, but Jesus wanted her to have an experience. Would it be possible for Martha to see beyond her sisterly squabble to hear what her Prince had to say? Only if she humbled herself enough to hear Jesus's caring words.

The Source of Peacelessness

Peacelessness is a state of being without quiet, calm, and order. Oh, we've all been there—when our list is longer than the time needed to accomplish even half the tasks. The resources are low and the demands are high. The hamster wheel has you trapped, dizzy, and nauseated. You stay up late and get up early, only to see things haven't changed overnight. A good night's sleep? Where do you get one of those? The anxieties and concerns continue to weigh us down. *If I could just get off this ride for a few minutes. If time could stand still, I …* (finish the sentence). Can you empathize with someone like Martha?

The only thing that will bring about change in Martha's life is to heed the words Jesus lovingly spoke to her. Isn't that true of you and me? Jesus's words give life. The words in the Bible give and preserve life. "This is my comfort in my affliction, for Your word has given me life" (Ps. 119:50 NKJV). If we would only listen and obey His Word, we'd experience the life He died to give us, a life full of peace, joy, and abundance.

Jesus is a gentleman. He has no history of violence or loud, over-bearing debates. His conversations are filled with love, kindness, and wisdom. He asks questions to make people think. So we have no reason to believe His words to Martha were meant to embarrass or condemn her. She was troubled; He knew why, and He wanted to help her, that's all. Let's examine His response again (Luke 10:41–42), but this time in another translation. Isn't it fun to study God's Word?!

> But the Lord answered her, "Martha, Martha, you are worried [anxious] and upset about many things. Only one thing is important [necessary; needed]. Mary has chosen the better thing, and it will never be taken away from her." (EXB)

Being distracted doesn't mean Martha was unspiritual; after all, she invited Jesus into her home. Busy girls know Jesus too. And being distracted is not a sin; it happens to all of us. However, when we read and understand these two verses together, we see that Martha had allowed her anxieties and worries to make her too busy. It wasn't just her to-do list that was the problem—her emotional reaction to the situation was keeping her from what was most important. Wow! Jesus can pack a lot into a few words, can't He?

✝ Our concerns, if not surrendered to our Prince, will steal our peace.

Being over-occupied and too busy has a ripple effect. Jesus identified Martha's state of mind; the source of her peacelessness was a troubled heart. Her busyness had caused anxiousness and worry. What were some of the many things she was worried about? I bet you can guess, can't you? We've all been there at some point or another. Trying to anticipate people's needs, trying to avoid any household disasters, responding to people's questions, making the best use of the resources available, wondering if everyone is doing what they should be doing, making sure everybody is comfortable—Martha may look like a flustered hostess, or a professional under pressure, or any mom on any given day. The combination of distraction, anxiety, and too much to do in too little time has the potential to cripple our spiritual growth. Our concerns, if not surrendered to our Prince, will steal our peace, unsettle our spirits, and keep us from experiencing the presence of God. We'll find ourselves grappling for anything that will provide some stability and balance.

When things begin to spin out of control, we often turn to the world for balance and stability. The world offers shiny, new, adventurous, systematic, and with-it ways to settle our restlessness and bring order to our lives. Calendars. Apps. Devices. Diets. Exercise. TED Talks. Podcasts. Programs. You name it, the world entices us with it. I'm not saying these things are bad, but they aren't the best. They aren't our Prince.

Ceasing Peacelessness: Part 1

What was Jesus's counsel to Martha? "Order your steps better, Martha. Do you have a calendar, Martha? I preached an excellent sermon series on this recently; you should listen to the podcast. Have you tried making lists and prioritizing your responsibilities? Lists are good."

Nope. His guidance wasn't to *do*, but to *sit*.

Jesus didn't use this specific word, but the inference is there in the conversation and in His remarks about Mary. Bible teacher Warren Wiersbe said, "Few things are as damaging to the Christian life as trying to work for Christ without taking time to commune with Christ."[2] I'm a great respecter of God's Word and would never violate its sanctity by adding my words to His, but in my mind, this is how I hear Jesus's response:

Dear Martha (as He gently touches her arm), the answers to all that concerns you are right here. (He points to a space beside Mary.) I know you've got so much on your mind, and the way you've handled things lately isn't working. You've separated yourself from what you know is right. My words are true. They give direction and instruction. Dinner can wait. Let's talk. I have exactly what you need.

✝ *Jesus's guidance wasn't
to do, but to sit.*

Jesus had the solution for Martha's distraction, her peacelessness: "Know Me." That's where we find peace, with Jesus. He was inviting her to really know Him, and this knowing goes beyond salvation. It's the knowing that Mary had. The sit-at-His-feet-and-have-a-little-talk knowing. It's the kind of knowing we have with only our bestest friends. But here's the thing: you can't know someone you don't spend time with, nor would you want to sit down with someone you don't really know.

My best friend is my best friend because we've spent over fifty years together. Sharing, shopping, swapping clothes, crying, fussing, helping, giving, laughing, listening, and learning from each other. It's all right that she drops by my house unexpectedly. (She's always invited.) When she comes in, I pause what I'm doing, and I sit down with her. I don't want to be distracted while we are visiting. She's important, and what she has to say is important.

Spending time every day with Jesus is how we get to know Him. While Mary most likely didn't see Jesus every day, she had spent enough time with Him to want to be sitting with Him more than doing anything else with any other person. When we are distracted, other things become more important, and we miss Jesus. We miss His teaching, His love, and His presence. Martha missed all of these. She was so busy worrying about the place settings that she forgot to take her place at His feet. She was so distracted by her sister's actions that she couldn't see what was "better."

When you know Jesus, you choose the better way. Let's you and I learn about that better way.

Mary: The Devoted Sister

In families with multiple children you can usually count on at least one child having horns and one having a halo. You know I'm right. (Are you thinking about your siblings and identifying the horn-wearer and halo-polisher?) I have a strong feeling Mary wore the halo in her family. The one with the halo makes the right decisions.

By her actions and Jesus's very own words, Mary was that girl. Let's refresh our minds with the two verses that bear her name.

> Her sister, Mary, sat at the Lord's feet, listening to what he taught. (Luke 10:39)

> There is only one thing worth being concerned about. Mary has discovered it, and it will not be taken away from her. (Luke 10:42)

We could call her a Goody Two-shoes and move on, but since name-calling isn't nice, let's hang out for a bit and get to know her. Why did she make the decision she did? Why was she sitting on the floor with Jesus instead of helping her sister with dinner? How could she sit and ignore the dinner preparations?

Mary was busy, but not like Martha. Mary was busy quieting her mind. Just as Martha had become unconsciously distracted, Mary had become intentionally focused. She sat at Jesus's feet with deliberate thought. She sat in humility and respect, to Jesus, and to the guests around her. She sat where she could hear Him best. She sat where He could see her and speak directly to her.

✝ Just as Martha had become unconsciously distracted, Mary had become intentionally focused.

There's more to sitting with Jesus than daydreaming or twiddling your thumbs. While we sit, we read the Bible, meditate on what it says, allow it to convict, heal, and open our eyes to see God in our midst.

I love the way Charles Spurgeon described sitting at Jesus's feet. Prepare yourself; Charles had a way with words. You might just end up on the floor.

> Imagine not that to sit at Jesus' feet is a very small, unmeaning thing. It means peace, for they who submit to Jesus find peace through his precious blood. It means holiness, for those who learn of Jesus learn no sin, but are instructed in things lovely and of good repute. It means strength, for they that sit with Jesus, and feed upon him, are girded with his strength; the joy of the Lord is their strength. It means wisdom, for they that learn of the Son of God understand more than the ancients, because they keep his statutes. It means zeal, for the love of Christ fires hearts that live upon it, and they that are much with Jesus become like Jesus, so that the zeal of the Lord's house eats them up.[3]

Mary knew Jesus. Her knowledge of His righteousness, goodness, grace, and mercy gave her peace. The peace passed all understanding, enabling her to sit rather than serve, to listen rather than labor.[4]

Ceasing Peacelessness: Part 1

"But few things are needed—or indeed only one. Mary has chosen what is better, and it will not be taken away from her" (Luke 10:42

NIV). Martha busied herself with lots of things. Mary focused on one thing—Jesus. I don't believe for one second that Jesus's statement meant that Mary neglected her domestic responsibilities or that she didn't have a social life. Scripture doesn't give us a lot of personal information about her, but since we know Mary put Jesus first, we can be fairly confident that she was a woman who ordered her life in such a way as to accomplish what needed to be accomplished and to fulfill her responsibilities. After all, Mary had most likely heard Jesus teach about loving others—we can guess that she was obedient to His commands. Mary was a woman devoted to God and Jesus Everlasting. It was because of this devotion that she chose what was better. And what is the better way?

To answer that question, we need to study a couple of words from Luke 10. *Better*, or maybe your translation uses the word *good*, is the Greek word *agathós*, and (from *Helps Word Studies*) it means "inherently (intrinsically) *good*; as to the believer, (*agathós*) describes what *originates from God* and is *empowered* by Him in their life, through faith."[5] Mary was good, however, not in her own nature, but because of her faith. Holding hands with the word *better* is *chosen*, and we can't overlook it. It's the Greek word *eklegó*, and (from *Helps Word Studies*) it means "to select (choose) out of, by a highly deliberate choice (i.e. real heart-preference) with a definite *out*come."[6] Mary's heart had been changed. The change led to an empowered life of faith that enabled her to know the right choice. Mary had the power to choose to sit instead of serve, because of Christ in her. You might say that "better" means empowered living through a relationship with Jesus Christ.

The choice Mary made was not only to sit in a place of humility but also to listen to Jesus. (Don't you wonder what He said?) As Dr.

Ralph F. Wilson pointed out in his JesusWalk Bible Studies, "That Jesus would encourage her to listen to him as he taught in the house was, in itself, radical. Women were openly despised by the Judaism of the time. Women were exempt from the study of the Torah. Many rabbis actively discouraged women from learning."[7]

Can you even imagine being discouraged from learning God's Word? God's Word is life to me. "I will never forget your commandments, for by them you give me life" (Ps. 119:93). What would your reaction be if someone told you that you could not know God's Word? My soul would grieve! Just the thought of it makes me heartsick.

Mary chose the better way. We don't know by what methods, but Mary had been a student of Jesus's teaching, and it's quite possible she studied or was taught the Torah. She esteemed Jesus and hung on His every word. Jesus's message silenced the complaints of her sister. Mary didn't get caught up in the chaos of the kitchen; her heart was at peace, because of her Prince.

It's important that we realize Mary's peace didn't start just in that moment. Peace isn't some magical, mystical emotion that settles on us like a cloud when everything around us is falling apart. Peace isn't experienced by placing a 911 prayer to God in the middle of pandemonium. The peace our Prince offers is generated through relationship, not panic. But can He instantly extend calm when trouble is stirred? Oh, yes, He can! He will always respond when His children press the panic button.

Remember when Jesus was on a boat with the disciples? All was well until a terrible storm came out of nowhere. The disciples, many of whom were experienced fishermen, panicked. Jesus? He was sleeping. Everything around Him was in great commotion, and Jesus was catching some *Zzzzz*. The disciples pressed the panic button. "Lord, save us! We're going to drown!" (Matt. 8:25). After a quick retort about their little faith, Jesus "rebuked the wind and waves, and suddenly there was a great calm" (v. 26). As Scott Krippayne sang, "Sometimes He calms the storm / And other times He calms His child."[8]

A calm is a temporary pause in the face of immediate discord, while peace is permanent no matter how severe the distress. But I'm not suggesting that even with the peace our Prince provides that we won't ever have trouble. Jesus said, "Here on earth you will have many trials and sorrows," and He also said, "But take heart, because I have overcome the world" (John 16:33). Our friend Jesus offers a peace that fills our hearts with so much love, trust, and faithfulness that when the unrest rises, we aren't overtaken by it. Mary knew this. Mary chose better. *How* did Mary choose better?

Mary "sat at the Lord's feet, listening to what he taught" (Luke 10:39). Will you underline the word *listening*? Martha was doing; Mary was listening. Again, busy girls can love Jesus, but we busy girls have a hard time listening when we are busy being busy. To Mary, it seemed to be the norm that she would go sit and listen to Jesus. There didn't appear to be an internal struggle pulling at her: kitchen versus King (or Prince). It seemed natural to her to go spend time with her Lord, teacher, friend, and confidant, even if it cost her something.

I mentioned my BFF earlier. Well, many years ago, we were allowed to talk on the phone only once a week. (Can you even imagine?!) She lived in the next county over and the call was long distance. In other words, it cost extra money. We could hardly wait for that weekly call! When I answered the phone each week, I knew it was Christie immediately, not because her number appeared on caller ID or because her picture popped up on the screen (rotary dial phones didn't have those features). I knew my best friend was on the other end because I recognized her voice. And I recognized her voice because I spent a lot of time with her.

Reading the Bible is how we hear from God and is an important way for us to spend time with God. His Spirit teaches us everything we need to know. "But when the Father sends the Advocate as my representative—that is, the Holy Spirit—he will teach you everything and will remind you of everything I have told you" (John 14:26). I love this verse! For some reason Christians are under the impression that since we are Christians, we should automatically know and understand everything the Bible says. Nothing is further from the truth. If this were true, then why would God send the Holy Spirit to teach us everything? We learn by listening. Mary had learned by listening to Jesus. This empowered her to choose better.

Akouó is the Greek word used for "listening." Its meaning is so simple: hearing, paying attention, considering, understanding, obeying.[9] Listening is more than only hearing. Listening is giving attention to what is being said with the intent to obey. In listening and learning, we not only get to know Jesus, but we also get to know ourselves. As we listen to God through reading His Word, we learn of His great love, receive guidance for living in a right relationship with Him, and see areas of our lives that need, well, a little adjusting. Through the love and wisdom of His Word, God reveals how to change our sinful ways and un-Christlike behavior. Hearing about areas in our lives that need correcting isn't easy, but it's necessary for us to be able to *choose better*. God loves us too much to leave us sinking in sinful living.

God isn't picking on us and being bossy. Correction comes from a heart of love and a desire to bring us in alignment with His best for our lives. Correction is redirection, not condemnation. I know it might sound odd, but God uses correction to create peace in our lives. Receiving both His love and His correction, then, generates the peace our hearts long for. We discover life isn't about hopping from one thing to the next, trying to figure out how to live fully in this up-and-down, roller-coaster-riding world. Peace comes through walking in the ways of the Lord and in constant fellowship with Him.

> ✝ *Correction is redirection,*
> *not condemnation.*

In surrendering to His ways, we are finally able to rest in the truth that He is the Prince of Peace and His peace is far superior to anything that the world offers or that we can manufacture. "I am leaving you with a gift—peace of mind and heart. And the peace I give is a gift the world cannot give" (John 14:27). This peace will steady you when the chaos seeks to overwhelm. It can be experienced in the midst of war, backbiting, racial tension, economic adversity, cultural unrest, and even a dinner party gone south. Jesus loved His friend Martha and was fully aware of the area of her life that needed adjusting. In love and with compassion, Jesus told Martha (this is how I hear it in my head), *It's right here, Martha; everything you need is right here. Sit right down beside Mary and listen.*

Is that what Jesus is saying to you right now?

Like the season finale of our favorite television show, we are left hanging. The story is suspended in time. Did Martha sit down beside Mary? Did she listen to Jesus's words and accept His correction? The story of the sisters continues in chapters 11 and 12 in the book of John, at another dinner party, a celebration of sorts. Oh, please read it on your own! The two chapters are riveting!

While that part of our story isn't wrapped in pretty paper and tied with ribbon, we can bring a close to this chapter with an exclamation point. We've read and reread Luke 10:42, but bear with me for a few minutes and take one more glance. I promise, it will be worth it.

Mary has chosen what is better, and it will not be taken away from her. (NIV)

Use your pen or highlighter to emphasize "it will not be taken away from her." Now pause and read the phrase out loud.

What Mary chose, what is better, could not be taken away. A life empowered by Jesus through faith in Jesus is permanent … here to stay. It was a certainty for Mary, and for everyone who has faith in Christ. He holds everyone with a tight grip. "I give them eternal life, and they will never perish. No one can snatch them away from me" (John 10:28). Nothing, not anything, can snatch us from His loving care. "And I am convinced that nothing can ever separate us from

God's love. Neither death nor life, neither angels nor demons, neither our fears for today nor our worries about tomorrow—not even the powers of hell can separate us from God's love" (Rom. 8:38).

Oh, please notice the phrase "nor our worries about tomorrow"! Christ is our Prince of Peace, friends, for yesterday's disappointments, today's defense, and tomorrow's dilemmas! Even our worries and concerns can't separate us from Jesus Everlasting. Can you even believe it?! I wish we could celebrate this good news together with a Jesus dance. We can live in permanent peace because of our Prince of Peace!

His peace gives us the

- assurance that even when everything around us isn't okay, everything will be okay;
- spiritual confidence to obey Him, even when it doesn't make sense; and
- courage to do what is right, even when others aren't.

What has stolen your peace? A broken or unfulfilled dream? Discouragement in a relationship? Limited finances? Uncertainty in your health? In Christ we can have peace in our hearts, even if we don't have peace in our circumstances. Seem impossible? The prophet Isaiah tells us exactly how: "You will keep in perfect peace all who trust in you, all whose thoughts are fixed on you!" (Isa. 26:3).

Set the table, then sit at His feet. When you know Jesus, you choose better. For everlasting!

Everlasting Thoughts

Remember, don't erase, edit, or omit. Just put pen or pencil to paper and listen to what God is trying to teach you through His Word right now.

When you think of peace, what comes to mind? Is it a place? Is it a person? Describe what peace means to you.

Don't worry—I won't make you take a Martha/Mary personality test. That's because I think all of us are a little like Martha and a little like Mary at various points in our lives. Make Martha and Mary columns down below. In each column, jot down some ways that you relate to either person.

What was the source of Martha's peacelessness? What is the source of your peacelessness?

In this chapter we looked at two parts to ceasing peacelessness. Write what you learned from those two parts—how can we gain peace?

Jesus acted as a friend to Martha and Mary in two surprising or unexpected ways. I'll give you a hint: one is by what He didn't do to Martha and one is by what He did allow for Mary. What are these two interesting responses from Jesus? Why would they have been unexpected at the time?

Sometime this week, read all of Isaiah 26. Write down here things you learn from the prophet's words about those who have or don't have peace.

When do you go to your friends to find peace? When do you go to your friend Jesus for peace? How are those times different or the same?

Leaning on the Music: "It Is Well with My Soul"

Words by Horatio Spafford, music
by Philip Bliss, 1876

How could a devoted Christian and prominent businessman who lost much of his fortune in the Great Chicago Fire of 1871 then later lost his four daughters in a shipwreck pen timeless words about peace and the wellness of his soul?

> When peace like a river, attendeth my way,
> When sorrows like sea billows roll
> Whatever my lot, thou hast taught me to say
> It is well, it is well, with my soul
>
> It is well
> With my soul
> It is well, it is well with my soul

It is said Horatio Spafford immersed himself in God's Word. A soul steeped in God's Word can be at peace when circumstances are not peaceful. Everyone is vulnerable to trouble and tragedy, even those with a deep, abiding faith. This doesn't seem fair, does it? Suffering is not a respecter of age, sex, creed, or of economic or social status.

I've said "That isn't fair" to God more times than I can count on all my fingers and toes. And truth be told, since I'm still breathing, I'm sure I'll say it again before He comes to get me. The truth is, we live in a fallen world, a world that is soaked in sin and self rather than in Scripture. Therefore, we will have heartache and times of peacelessness, but we don't have to abide in them. Even though it may often be the last place we turn, Scripture is the treatment for troubled times.

Peacelessness has many causes. Grief over the passing of a loved one, the loss of a job, or the end of a relationship can plunge us into dark, weary times. But perhaps less obvious are the turmoil and stress caused by social media posts, by the person who pulled out in front of us on the way to work, or by a certain number on the bathroom scale. Societal injustices, the state of the national economy, lawlessness, and civil unrest are all examples of things that can get under our skin like a bur under a saddle. The poor horse saddled by any of the above is going to buck, kick, and whinny until something is done and calm can be restored.

I've been there. I've bucked, kicked, screamed, and acted like a fool concerning things that stole my peace. I've treated my aching heart with shopping trips, movie bingeing, gardening, and redecorating. And here's what I know: our peace is up to us and is directly related to that which we choose to consume.

It's a matter of what we choose to surrender to—will we surrender to the noise and chaos of the world or to the Prince of Peace? It's a matter of what we put in our souls—will we feed on the ills and corruption of the enemy's stomping grounds or on the truth and hope of the Living God?

His peace, the peace of Christ, is an abiding peace that stays with us even when the greatest sorrows, like sea billows, roll our way. It's a peace that gives hope and assurance of a life to come, no matter what our lots in this life might be. It's a peace that comforts us in our loss and reminds us that we will be restored. Imagine, as some accounts say, Horatio traveling to meet his wife who survived the shipwreck, and passing close to the spot where his daughters had died, and being inspired by God to write the words of this song, which has gone on to remind thousands and thousands of people about the peace that comes only through Christ and allows us to feel well in our souls, even when nothing seems right. Think about Horatio longing to see his children again and writing these words:

> And Lord, haste the day when the faith
> > shall be sight,
> The clouds be rolled back as a scroll;
> The trump shall resound, and the Lord
> > shall descend,
> Even so, it is well with my soul.

Our friend Mary's soul was well. She knew this peace. Mary was able to sit at the feet of Jesus, listening to His words, despite the chaos going on around her. We can do the same. We can spend time sitting with Jesus, reading His Word, and be reminded, day after day, that He knows the causes of our heartache and He sees the stress we are under. And He will make things right. If we choose the better way, His peace will not be taken from us, no matter what.

Chapter 6

The Sweetest Name I Know

There's within my heart a melody;
Jesus whispers sweet and low,
"Fear not, I am with you, peace, be still,"
in all of life's ebb and flow.

I believe we all long for a sweet melody in our hearts, don't you? A song of assurance and love that says, "Don't be afraid. You have peace; just be still." The tune you can sing when life's ebb and flow threaten to wash you away. Luther Bridgers had such a melody. Luther not only sang the song, but he also wrote the song.

A native North Carolinian and the son of a preacher, Luther answered the Lord's call on his life at seventeen. After attending what was then known as Asbury College (in Wilmore, Kentucky), he spent his life as a pastor and evangelist in the Methodist Episcopal Church. He married a girl named Sarah, whom he met at college, and the Lord blessed them with three sons. Luther was a well-known evangelist at the time and was often asked to preach the gospel in surrounding towns.

The year after "He Keeps Me Singing" was published, Luther was away from home on a preaching trip when his wife and children went to visit her parents. Sometime in the night, the home caught on fire. Neighbors came to help, but Luther's wife and three sons did not make it out.[1] Some of the song's lines seem to echo the writer's suffering: "All my life was wrecked by sin and strife, discord filled my heart with pain" and "Sometimes He leads through waters deep, trials fall across the way." But no matter what happened, Luther relied on Jesus to help him get through it:

> Jesus, Jesus, Jesus,
> sweetest name I know,
> fills my every longing,
> keeps me singing as I go.

When I started writing *Jesus Everlasting*, this refrain began playing in my mind and has been playing ever since: *Jesus, Jesus, Jesus, sweetest name I know.* I grew up singing hymns and have a great love for them. This one has always been one of my favorites, even more so now that I know some of the story of the songwriter.

How do we sing the song of Jesus? Do we have to experience a tragedy before we can know its harmony and belt out the lyrics? I don't think so; however, it is through life's ebb and flow that we get to know Him as our Wonderful Counselor, Mighty God, Everlasting Father, and Prince of Peace. Luther *knew* the song of Jesus before he experienced the tragedy. His was a life surrendered to that melody. He lived it. And when that fire took his family, it could not steal Luther's song.

✝ *Breathe in the name of Jesus.*
Breathe out the name of Jesus.

Will you take a few minutes to say His name out loud several times? Speak it over your current circumstances and over the past that still attempts to choke the life out of you and over the future that seems so uncertain. Breathe in the name of Jesus. Breathe out the name of Jesus. Ahh. His name makes everything fade away, doesn't it? His name makes you smile. He is the song that keeps His children going all day long.

We've studied Jesus's beautiful interactions with five women. Hasn't it been lovely to see how He values and esteems women? It's fitting that we conclude our time together by delving into each story one last time, looking in these stories for hints of what our next steps might be. Remember that Jesus has always been, is now, and will always be the answer for everything we need. Let's add our voices to the song of Jesus and keep singing about and leaning on our Wonderful Counselor, Mighty God, Everlasting Father, and Prince of Peace.

She Told Everyone

I have always loved going to church—toting my Bible, a notebook, and a highlighter. Even when I was younger and didn't really know much about being a Christian, I loved going to church, carrying my Bible, and putting my envelope in the offering plate.

These days, offerings are often handled electronically, but back then my church mailed out giving envelopes each month to every church member. I LOVED getting mail and having my name on something! I'll go ahead and admit it: I wasn't a fan of giving some of my babysitting money to the church, but I've come around about that (a story for another day). The envelope wasn't just about giving, though; it was also about accountability.

In addition to the space to write the amount you were giving, there were several little checkboxes beside accountability statements, or at least that's what I call them. Maybe you can picture what I'm talking about. The checkboxes were the members' opportunities to share how they had grown or stretched their faith during the week.

- ☐ Studied Sunday school lesson
- ☐ Bible brought to church
- ☐ Bible read daily
- ☐ Invited someone to church
- ☐ Witnessed to others

Oh, how my heart wanted to check all those boxes so my church would be proud of me. I could check some, but not all. The box beside "Witnessed to others" was always left blank. So I felt sure the envelope-opener people would tell my pastor that my boxes were not all checked and they'd revoke my membership.

Sharing with someone about how to become a Christian intimidated me. I had very little confidence in myself about life in general, much less about Bible stuff. *What if they asked me questions about the Bible that I couldn't answer? What if they wanted me to look up a scripture in Ezra? Where is Ezra anyway? Who is Ezra? And what about the second coming and judgment day?* The questions paralyzed the zeal of my salvation.

Lack of spiritual confidence and inability to answer questions might be understandable excuses for a young girl not to share her faith. But let's face it: even many of those who have journeyed with Jesus for a long time are fearful of sharing their faith. However, every believer should be able to tell about his or her relationship with God through His Son, Jesus. "If someone asks about your hope as a believer, always be ready to explain it" (1 Pet. 3:15). We don't have to fear; we just have to tell.

The woman at the well didn't preach a sermon on the steps of the temple, write her story down in a book of memoirs, or attend seminary to be schooled in the Scriptures before she became a witness-telling believer. She simply told everyone what Jesus did for her, and "many Samaritans from the village believed in Jesus because the woman had said, 'He told me everything I ever did!'" (John 4:39).

Evangelism, or telling the good news about Jesus, isn't really an option for believers. "Sing to the LORD; praise his name. Each day proclaim the good news that he saves. Publish his glorious deeds among the nations. Tell everyone about the amazing things he does. Great is the LORD! He is most worthy of praise! He is to be feared above all gods" (Ps. 96:2–4). Our responsibility, no, our privilege, is to tell about Jesus.

✝ *If we exercise our privilege, God*
will silence all the what-ifs.

Often, we are afraid to go tell because of the what-ifs mentioned earlier. If we exercise our privilege, God will silence all the what-ifs. He gives us confidence to be okay not to have all the answers. Just think about when you come across a good article or a great product—don't you feel the need to share it with someone? Or with everyone on social media? You don't let the fact that you don't know every detail stop you. You just want to share the good thing you've found. "The LORD our God has secrets known to no one. We are not accountable for them, but we and our children are accountable forever for all that he has revealed to us, so that we may obey all the terms of these instructions" (Deut. 29:29).

Friends, we don't have all the answers, nor do we have the power to save. "For I am not ashamed of this Good News about Christ. It is the power of God at work, saving everyone who believes—the Jew first and also the Gentile" (Rom. 1:16). Salvation belongs to our God; planting the seeds of the gospel in the heart of anyone who will listen is up to us.

Don't let the churchy sound of the word *evangelism* frighten you. It's true, evangelism can be radical and bold. It can mean going door to door with pamphlets that outline verses about salvation. It can mean traveling across the globe to a remote part of the world with a translator. But it can also mean living a holy and righteous life among nonbelievers with the desire to draw them to Jesus Christ. The woman at the well chose the personal approach. She ran from the well to the town and told what Jesus did for her. She was so excited, she couldn't *not* tell. God had saved her and set her free from the bondage of a broken life.

Has He saved you? Then tell someone; tell everyone: Jesus saves!

She Was Convicted

In John 8, after all the accusing men had left, Jesus asked the woman caught in adultery if any one of them had condemned her. Her answer was, "No, Lord." Jesus's reply was almost as brief, but amazingly bold: "Neither do I. Go and sin no more" (v. 11).

The unfortunate part of this story is that we don't hear of our unnamed friend again. We don't know if she left her life of sin behind. We do know, however, that Jesus came to her defense and sent her off with the hope of a new beginning. It's the same new beginning Paul told the Corinthians about: "This means that anyone who belongs to Christ has become a new person. The old life is gone; a new life has begun" (2 Cor. 5:17). When we encounter Christ and experience the power of His forgiveness, we are a new creation, with a new future full of hope.

Some may suggest that Jesus wasn't harsh enough with this woman. He didn't quote Scripture or exact punishment according to the law. However, He did deal with her sin. Jesus didn't excuse her sin; He freed her from it. His words weren't condemning; they were convicting and liberating. As Paul explained to the Romans, "Therefore, there is now no condemnation for those who are in Christ Jesus" (Rom. 8:1 NIV).

When we sin, the Spirit of God convicts us of our sin; that's His job. Conviction says in our hearts: *Hey. That's not in alignment with God's Word. It's not His best for your life. It's wrong. Tell Jesus you are sorry. Receive His forgiveness, turn from the sin, and never do it again. He loves you.* Conviction offers us a choice and encourages us to respond.

Condemnation, on the other hand, ends our opportunity to choose and births shame instead of change. Condemnation speaks words of despair: *Hey. You're a loser. You can't stay out of trouble. You call yourself a Christian, but you keep sinning the same sin over and over again. He won't forgive you this time. You really can't help it; this is just who you are.*

> ✝ Conviction offers us a choice and encourages us to respond.

Maybe you are a visual learner like me, and picturing in your mind the phrases below will help further clarify the distinctions. This is a helpful chart I shared in my book *Yes, No, and Maybe: Living with the God of Immeasurably More*. Notice that conviction looks up at Jesus for hope, love, forgiveness, and reconciliation, while condemnation looks down in shame, disgrace, and humiliation.

Condemnation	Conviction
Looks down in remembering	Looks up and rejoices
Looks down in regret	Looks up with relief
Looks down in guilt	Looks up in gratitude
Looks down in despair	Looks up with hope
Looks forward with doubt	Looks forward with optimism

The fact is, Christians need to let go of condemnation because Jesus has freed us from it. To say otherwise would be to undermine the power of Christ. And there isn't a sin we will commit that God cannot forgive. The greatest example of this is Paul, who was the single most influential evangelical voice in all of the New Testament. But before he was Paul the soul winner, he was Saul the murderer and persecutor of all Christians. We can't out-sin God's forgiveness; it's impossible.

Jesus has a long history of forgiveness. "God is faithful and reliable. If we confess our sins, he forgives them and cleanses us from everything we've done wrong" (1 John 1:9 GW). But while it's impossible to out-sin God's grace, it is also impossible for us in our current state not to sin. We were born with a sinful nature, in need of forgiveness. Jesus was born with a perfect nature, ready to offer forgiveness.

So why did He tell the woman to sin no more? The word Jesus used for "sin" in John 8 is the Greek word *hamartane*, which isn't even specifically for the sin of adultery but rather a word referring to all sin. Jesus was offering the woman both a challenge and a hope. "Go and sin no more." Change your life. Start new. Not because you can on your own power, but because you can through Christ.

When we walk in right relationship with Jesus (reading His Word, praying, and obeying what He asks us to do), sin will be become offensive to us. And when we do sin, we won't be able to stand ourselves until we confess and receive forgiveness. Kind of like when you've been working in the yard all day; you're hot, sweaty, covered in dirt, and you can't wait to jump in a cool shower to get cleaned off. Confession is the cool shower that cleans you from sin. We will keep sinning, and Jesus will keep forgiving. However, it's the hope of Christ and our hope in Christ that as we tarry here on this earth, the sin in our lives decreases.

Jesus knew this woman would sin again, but He gave her the hope that she could live a different kind of life—a life free from condemnation and founded on forgiveness. The more we heed the Spirit's quickness in our spirits and seek the power of our Mighty God, the more strength we will have to sin no more.

She Followed Him

Yes, I'll follow Him forever! What person whose sins have been forgiven and is living in total freedom because of Jesus wouldn't follow Him? We emphatically say, "Yes, and amen!" Following the Lord, wherever He leads, sounds good … until He leads us to the edge of the world to a place not found on Google Earth. We raise our hands and say, "Pick me! Pick me!" But what about when the road leads to a cross?

Let's sit here for a minute and take that in: Would you follow Him forever if forever leads to death? Would Jesus really ask us to follow Him to such a place? Boy, we are going deep, friends: the answer is yes.

Wait! Doesn't He care? Doesn't He see I have family and know I have dreams? Oh, yes! He sees all that concerns His children. Moreover, He knows all things about His children. "And the very hairs on your head are all numbered" (Matt. 10:30). He knows the good work you will accomplish for the kingdom. "For we are God's masterpiece. He has created us anew in Christ Jesus, so we can do the good things he planned for us long ago" (Eph. 2:10). He knows all about our days on this earth, from our beginning to our end. "You saw me before I was born. Every day of my life was recorded in your book. Every moment was laid out before a single day had passed" (Ps. 139:16). He knows we in our human bodies are finite. "How do you know what your life will be like tomorrow? Your life is like the morning fog—it's here a little while, then it's gone" (James 4:14).

> † *"If you give up your life for my sake, you will save it."*

But Jesus is everlasting. "Before the mountains were born or You gave birth to the earth and the world, even from everlasting to everlasting, You are God" (Ps. 90:2 NASB).

We are but a frame in the film of eternity. Everything God does and asks us to do pertains to the greater vision He sees. I know it's a bit of a bummer to talk about death and our lives being like a morning fog, but then again, as weird as it might sound, this chatter should not only create an excitement in our spirits but also an urgency. God has a plan for us, one created long ago, and we only have a short time to fulfill it.

Mary Magdalene followed Jesus from the place where He freed her of the seven demons to the cross, and then to the tomb. Mary left her life to follow Jesus. She said no to her wants, whims, and wishes. She exchanged "me and mine" for "You and Yours." In fact, she was privy to a great teaching on this very subject. Jesus gave an excellent illustration of exactly what "follow me" means. We touched on this verse briefly in chapter 4.

> Then he said to the crowd, "If any of you wants to be my follower, you must give up your own way, take up your cross daily, and follow me. If you try to hang on to your life, you will lose it. But if you give up your life for my sake, you will save it." (Luke 9:23–24)

The cross is a symbol of Christ's love for us. We wear it around our necks and have it inked on our ankles, embossed on our Bibles, and airbrushed on our T-shirts. But to this crowd, the cross meant death. This message was intense! Maybe they even whispered to each other: "Wait, what? Did He say what I think He said? I have to carry a cross? If I want to follow Him, I have to die?" Carrying a cross always led to *death* on a cross; Mary knew this. No one carried a cross for fun.

The first hearers of Jesus didn't need an explanation of the cross; they knew what it meant—punishment, torture, and death. Taking up a cross was like buying a one-way ticket. And in first-century Rome, no one *took up* a cross voluntarily. Crosses were *placed on* people who were forced to carry them until they collapsed from exhaustion. So here, in His words to His disciples, Jesus was asking them to be willing to put their lives on the line to follow Him. To be all in.[2]

Jesus used the word *daily* to help His audience understand this was a spiritual application, not necessarily a physical requirement.

However, there are many who have died as a result of following Jesus. Stephen, Andrew, and Simon Peter all died for the cause of Christ. But Christ's disciples didn't die just in the first century. Meet a few others who followed Christ to the cross:

- William Tyndale: a church reformer who is best known for his translation of the Bible into English using the original languages, he died while tied to the stake, and then his body was burned, noted on October 6, 1536.
- Jim Elliot and four other missionaries: these men were killed on January 8, 1956, while trying to establish contact and bring the gospel to the Auca Indians in Ecuador.
- Nag Hammadi Massacre: a group of eight Egyptian Christians were killed as they left their church after celebrating a Christmas mass in Nag Hammadi, Egypt, on January 7, 2010.[3]

Every follower of Christ is a disciple. A *disciple* is "a follower of Christ who learns the doctrines of Scripture and the lifestyle they require."[4] While every Christian is a disciple, not everyone who follows Christ will experience the same fate as the aforementioned martyrs. Remember, Jesus was speaking metaphorically; you can't physically die daily, but you can symbolically surrender your life to God and His Word.

Christian author Louie Giglio called this lifestyle "a daily funeral." He went on to say a daily funeral "is nothing more than the doorway to a life filled with the matchless wonder of all that God is."[5] The apostle Paul, from a prison cell, facing death, wrote, "For to me, living means living for Christ, and dying is even better" (Phil. 1:21). We might not be faced with giving our physical lives for Christ, but we have great gain awaiting if we choose to die to self and follow Jesus. B. B. McKinney composed a beautiful hymn that includes these lyrics: "Wherever He leads I'll go / Wherever He leads I'll go. I'll follow my Christ who loves me so / Wherever He leads I'll go." Search online for the hymn. It's worth the listen.

Jesus loved Mary Magdalene and all of His disciples. Jesus loves you too! Will you follow your Everlasting Father wherever He leads?

She Listened

Boy, did I dread report card day when I was a kid. I'm a talker, always have been. It never failed; every grading period, every teacher wrote the letter C beside the word *Conduct*. Let me clarify: the C didn't represent the word *Conduct*. C was defined as "needs improvement," and it was my grade. My sweet teachers would write comments like, "Wendy is very social," "Wendy is a busy girl," "Wendy could learn more if she talked less." As hard as I tried, I could not keep my mouth shut.

I wish I could say that I've changed. If you were to put me and my besties in a room, we'd literally talk all night. We'd talk about everything, then we'd talk about everything again, eat, then talk some more. As a Christian speaker, talking is what I do. I'm very grateful God can use this skill set for His glory. However, sometimes God wants me to be quiet and to listen, like Mary, who sat at the Lord's feet (Luke 10:39).

A few years ago, my special skill became a stumbling block in my quiet times with Jesus. I found myself filling the time with words, lots of words. I felt it necessary to offer God possible solutions to all the circumstances in my life. If there happened to be a moment of silence, I'd write a to-do list in my head rather than sit quietly. The dusty shelves and piles of stuff distracted me. I wonder if the Son ever said to the Father, "I can't get a word in edgewise with this girl!"

✝ *Everything He has to say is worthwhile.*

I sensed multiple times the Spirit telling me to be silent, but silence is difficult for a chatterbox like me, so I ignored the prompting. After many mornings of the same urging, I acknowledged to the Lord what I was sensing and how uneasy silence made me feel. I still remember the tenderness in the response I felt Him give me: "Shhh. Be still. It's okay to be silent. You don't have to say a word." Over time the apprehension about being quiet was overcome by peace. I grew to love just sitting on the floor, by His feet. (At least that's how I thought of it.) I learned a very valuable lesson during my season of silence: you can't listen if you're always talking.

We learned earlier that we are all disciples, and a disciple is a follower of Christ who learns and lives out obedience to the Scriptures. In order to listen well, we have to be still and silent, like Mary. Listening demonstrates love and respect and honor. "Be still, and know that I am God! I will be honored by every nation. I will be honored throughout the world" (Ps. 46:10).

All of Mary's attention was on Jesus, the only one who had anything worth saying. You know, it grieves my heart to think of what I might have missed because I didn't keep my mouth closed and listen more intently during my morning quiet times with the Lord. Did He want to share something through His Word that would spare me pain? Was the devotional a tool to prepare me for an event that would occur that day, only I was in too big of a hurry to hear?

In a world where screens and digital distractions seem preferred over silence, sitting still has to be practiced. It's a discipline, something that takes time and dedication to achieve, especially for women like me who prefer to talk and hurry things along. God speaks through His Word and teaches through His Spirit. Everything He has to say is worthwhile. Mary knew this. She listened to Him and experienced the peace that goes beyond anything we can understand (Phil. 4:7).

Where Can I Meet Jesus Now?

It's easy to read about these women and be temporarily inspired by their actions, and even adopt those actions as our next steps, but then be tempted into thinking, *Those women were in the Bible, and Jesus physically, spiritually, and emotionally touched them. Of course they were changed!* Oh, please, don't put Jesus Everlasting on your bookshelf and believe you can't experience Jesus the same way as our Bible friends did. It's true, we aren't able to touch Him physically, but we can still experience Him, every moment of every day, through the presence of His Spirit living in us. Just meet Him like all our friends did.

At the Well

Where do you go to get refreshment? Where or what is your well? For many years my well was any kind of shopping. If there was a doorbuster, I had to get it; if there was a coupon, I had to use it. But shopping left me thirsty—literally and figuratively. It was like the water the Samaritan woman was going to retrieve from the well that Jesus said would leave her thirsty for more. But He had a solution in mind. And He's got something for you too. Look for Jesus at your well; I know He's looking for you. He wants to fill you with love, grace, and mercy like you've never known. After being with Him awhile, you will never again desire what the well offers. In fact, you will run to others and tell them all about what Jesus did for you.

At the Point of Shame

The Lord longs to defend you from accusers and forgive your sin. He intercedes with God on your behalf and pleads your case. "Therefore he is able, once and forever, to save those who come to God through him. He lives forever to intercede with God on their behalf" (Heb. 7:25). He is your Mighty God, in charge of heaven's armies, and He will not hesitate to stand in your defense. Get real with yourself and be honest about the ways you have hurt others or disobeyed God. Stop living in fear of being caught and waiting for the stones to fly.

When you humble yourself before Jesus, He will send you away, free to live a new life with the desire to sin no more.

At the Cross

Daily dying is great gain, because when we decrease, He increases (John 3:30). Each day we have the opportunity to put Him first, to see Him at work and join Him. He's there when the man doesn't have enough money to buy lunch. You can see Him in the faces of your children when they ask to stop at the park on the way home from school. He can be experienced as you prepare the medication boxes for your momma, who can no longer do it herself. In any moment where you feel yourself saying "Someone should really do something about that" or "That's out of my comfort zone," check your hands and your heart. Where's your cross? Where is Jesus asking you to die to self and live for Him? He can be seen and experienced *if* we carry the cross rather than just wear it around our necks.

At His Feet

Oh, this is the best place to be. It sets the tone of our relationship with our Lord. Taking a position at His feet reminds us (in case we ever forget!) that we are not His equal. "You are God and I am not. You are in charge of everything; my job is to listen and obey. You are the great One and I am your servant. You are the Father and I am the child." There's so much to learn sitting quietly at His feet. We just have to slow down long enough to take our place. Have you made time for Him in your day? He's waiting for us, ready to share everything we need to know. And ready to give us peace.

Dear friend, never forget that Jesus Everlasting is the Son given to us—gifted to us in an unexpected way to bless us for all time. He may surprise us with what He knows about us. He may challenge us by standing with us, forcing us to stand up taller than we knew we could. He may call to us in a place we never expected to meet Him. He may stop us in our tracks and lay out some truth for us. But He will always be there for us, every minute, every day, every year, for everlasting.

He was not the Rescuer the Israelites of old were looking for, but He is the Rescuer we need. His counsel is more about surrender than shrewdness, and He asks us to love our enemies instead of fight them. He left us all on purpose, and many thought He was gone for good. And the peace He offered seemed to come only at a high price—the cost of a life of sacrifice. But what the Israelites could not see, He has shown us in His Word and continues to teach us every day. He is the better gift, the best gift, in fact, that can never be taken away. And I'm so glad we have eternity to unwrap all the treasures He has for us. Aren't you?

Everlasting Thoughts

Remember, don't erase, edit, or omit. Just put pen or pencil to paper and listen to what God is trying to teach you through His Word right now.

In this chapter we talk about four ways the women in Jesus's stories sang the song of Jesus, ways that we can also use to get to know Him better. What are those four ways?

Which of those ways stands out to you as being something you long to do? Which one stands out as being something you are afraid to do? Explain your answer.

At the end of the chapter, we look at four places we can go to meet Jesus: at the well, at the point of shame, at the cross, and at His feet. The well represents a place we go to get fueled up, but where we are left unsatisfied. The point of shame is a place where we have to face our sins. The cross is a place where we have to die to self. And at His feet is a place where we learn to be still. Pick one of these places and think about what you would have to do to meet Jesus there. What might you have to give up? What might you need to be honest with yourself about? Be as specific as you can.

When we think about Jesus being everlasting, we may naturally think about Him existing for eternity, with no ending and no beginning. But realizing that Jesus is everlasting means understanding that He has always known us too and that He always will. He will always be with us. Right here with us—in our struggles and triumphs, in our ugly moments and when our beauty shines. Read Psalm 139 this week and write down here all the ways you notice these verses telling us Jesus is with us—yesterday, today, and tomorrow. Pick one special phrase to remember and serve as your reminder of Jesus Everlasting.

Leaning on the Music: "There Was Jesus"

Words and music by Zach Williams, Casey
Beathard, and Jonathan Smith, 2019

"It's about the reflection," said Zach Williams about his mega hit
"There Was Jesus." "I'm looking back at twenty years ago, where I
had no idea that God was in the moment, that He was even, you
know, with me through some of the things that had gone on in my
life. But looking back now, I can see that He had His hand in everything I was doing."[6]

Reflection—it's a double-edged sword, isn't it? Reflecting on our
past can be painful and heartbreaking; however, it can also be com-
forting and heart-lifting. The response depends on our focus. Are we
looking *at* our disappointments or *for* God's directing in our lives?

I look back to the ICU waiting room filled with thirty to forty
people praying when we thought my momma wouldn't make it
through the night. And in another hospital, years later, when we
thought her life would end while fighting cancer. Then there was the

time my father broke his leg and was unable to work, and food showed up on our back porch and cashier's checks filled our mailbox.

Jesus was there.

Fast-forward to when my husband, Scott, endured an undiagnosed illness for eighteen months and almost lost sight in one eye. Later, Scott was out of work. We had one child in college, the other in private school. Yet our cabinets had food, our cars were filled with gas, and the power was never turned off.

Jesus was there.

I can imagine our new friends we've walked with in this book would all have the same response if they could tell us their stories— Jesus was there. Yes, He did interact with each woman here on earth, but the relationships formed before Calvary most certainly continued after the ascension. How do I know? Because once you've encountered the presence of the Living God, you can't return to life as normal.

Jesus is ALWAYS there. He will never leave or forsake us, not ever.

God shows up! Every time and on time. He is never *not* with us. He is Jesus Everlasting. There is no beginning or end to Him; He showers endless love and boundless grace on His children. As time slips away, and we end our time together, dare to reflect back on your life—not to see the pain, but to see His presence.

There was Jesus. As the song says, Jesus is there "in the waiting, in the searching, in the healing and the hurting." Even when we think He doesn't see us. Even when we think He wouldn't possibly want to stand with us. Even when we can't hear Him calling us. Even when we can't imagine feeling His peace. He was, and is, and for everlasting will be your Counselor, Defender, Father, and Friend. Lean on Him.

Epilogue

My husband and I have been married for twenty-eight years (at the writing of this book). He is an excellent gift giver. Over our years together, he has really spoiled me. Yes, there have been unique pieces of jewelry and perfume. He loves to select a new fragrance for me. He has attempted to buy clothes, and well, let's just say that didn't work out too well. He fills my stocking at Christmas with gift cards to my favorite places to eat. I've loved all his gifts (well, maybe not the clothes), but one gift stands out as the best ever, with the exception of my engagement ring.

Before I just blurt out the gift, let me build the story a bit, so when I tell you the name of the gift you don't immediately think, *Oh. Way to go, Scott. Every girl loves a domestic treasure like that.* (There you go; you have a little hint.)

To go back in time a bit, let me tell you that one of my favorite things to do as a little girl was to lick the batter when my mom was baking. It didn't matter what sweet treat she was preparing: homemade Congo Squares, store-bought brownie mix, or my favorite—a simple vanilla pound cake. Is your mouth watering yet? Mine is.

Simple may not be the best way to describe a pound cake. The rich buttery vanilla confectionary is simple and smooth in taste yet complex and time-consuming in preparation. (And all the bakers say, "Amen!") The secret to a smooth and delicious pound cake is in the mixing. Each ingredient has to be mixed in slowly and thoroughly. Rushing will ruin a cake. Here are some of the highlights of the process. (For my momma and grandmomma's complete recipe, keep reading until the end of the book.)

- Blend smoothly 2 sticks of butter, the Crisco, and sugar.
- Beat 5 eggs, adding one at time.
- Add flour and milk alternately.
- Always use real vanilla—imitations won't do.

You can imagine how long this takes. Take a minute and picture me standing there in my kitchen, gathering ingredients, measuring them out, getting the hand mixer out, mixing each ingredient in bit by bit, then putting the mixer down, getting the next thing, mixing it in, then stopping again, and so forth. I couldn't even count how many times the mixer must be turned on and off through the whole process. Baking a pound cake is something I love to do for my family, but make no mistake—it is a job. It takes time. It takes attention. And it takes a lot of mixing.

Now, my sweet husband LOVES my pound cakes and appreciates the labor of love that is involved in making them. So one year for Christmas, his gift showed me just how much he appreciated me.

Sometimes a girl's best gifts come in the smallest packages, and sometimes they don't. That particular year, my best gift was in a very large and extremely heavy box. As I peeled back the paper, I could

read the label. I squealed like a schoolgirl whose crush just asked
her to the prom. My guy had been watching my labor of love for
many years and decided to make my life better by … giving me a
KitchenAid stand mixer.

Yes! There are times when a domestic gift beats any treasure con-
cealed in a small velvet jewelry box.

It's been more than fifteen years since I opened that heavy box,
and cake baking hasn't been the same since. Each time I pull the
mixer from the shelf, I think of Scott and how thoughtful his gift
was. In fact, I often call him or send a text telling him how much I
still appreciate this gift. The mixer is a gift that keeps on giving.

Over two thousand years ago, the world was given a matchless
gift in the person of Jesus, a present that was prophesied seven hundred years prior to His arrival. He was and still is the hope of the
world. He is our Counselor, Defender, Father, and Friend, and we
can always lean on Him. He is the gift that keeps on giving. He is
Jesus Everlasting.

Pound Cake (Happy Baking!)

Ingredients

1 cup (sticks) softened unsalted butter

½ cup butter-flavor Crisco (plus extra for the pan)

3 cups sugar

5 eggs (beat and add one at a time)

3 cups plain flour (plus extra for the pan)

½ teaspoon salt

½ teaspoon baking powder

1 cup milk

1 tablespoon pure vanilla extract

Instructions

Classic cake recipe:

1. Grease and flour a pound cake loaf pan and set it aside.
2. Blend butter, Crisco, and sugar together on high speed until light and fluffy.

3. Add 1 egg at a time until all 5 are mixed in.

4. Stir salt and baking powder with flour in a separate bowl.

5. Stir dry mixture and milk slowly into the butter and sugar mixture, alternating between adding the flour and milk until all is combined well.

6. Stir in vanilla flavoring.

7. Pour batter into prepared loaf pan.

8. Bake at 400 degrees (F) for 10 minutes, then at 325 for 1 hour. When a toothpick inserted in the center of the cake comes out clean, the cake is ready. Take it out and let it cool.

Breakfast recipe:

1. Prepare batter as shown above. When batter is ready, pour ½ in the loaf pan.

2. Mix together 1 cup finely chopped pecans, 1 cup brown sugar, and 4 tablespoons of cinnamon in a separate bowl.

3. Put spoonfuls of half of the cinnamon mixture on top of the batter in the loaf pan. Use a knife to swirl the mixture around.

4. Pour in remaining batter. Add the rest of the cinnamon mixture and swirl it into the batter again.

5. Bake in same manner as mentioned above.

Notes

Chapter 1: A Son Who Was Given to Us

1. "The History of 'Hallelujah' Chorus from *Handel's Messiah*," *Tabernacle Choir* (blog), Tabernacle Choir at Temple Square, February 22, 2016, www .thetabernaclechoir.org/articles/history-of-handels-hallelujah-chorus.html.

2. "His Name—The Mighty God," sermon in *Sermons Preached and Revised by the Rev. C. H. Spurgeon*, vol. 6 (New York: Sheldon, 1860), 142–43.

3. Justin Holcomb, "What Is Grace?," Christianity.com, January 23, 2013, www.christianity.com/theology/what-is-grace.html.

Chapter 2: A Counselor Who Knows Us

1. "Old and New Testament Greek Lexicon Dictionary," *Mounce*, s.v. "γυναικάριον," StudyLight.org, accessed January 4, 2021, www.studylight .org/lexicons/greek/1133.html.

2. "Old and New Testament Greek Lexicon Dictionary," *Mounce*, s.v. "δᾶ," StudyLight.org, accessed January 4, 2021, www.studylight.org/lexicons /greek/1163.html.

3. *Thayer's Greek Lexicon*, s.v. "zaó," Bible Hub, accessed January 4, 2021, https://biblehub.com/thayers/2198.htm.

4. David Guzik, "John 4—A Samaritan Woman and a Nobleman Meet Jesus," *Enduring Word Bible Commentary*, accessed January 4, 2021, https://enduringword.com/bible-commentary/john-4/.

Chapter 3: A Defender Who Stands with Us

1. "What Does the Bible Mean When It Calls God the 'LORD of Hosts'?," Got Questions, accessed January 5, 2021, www.gotquestions.org/Lord-of-hosts .html.

2. *The Tony Evans Bible Commentary* (Nashville: Holman Bible Publishers, 2019), 1233.

Chapter 4: A Father Who Calls to Us

1. C. H. Spurgeon, *The Treasury of the Old Testament*, vol. 3 (Grand Rapids, MI: Zondervan, 1951), 441.

2. *Thayer's Greek Lexicon*, s.v. "diakoneó," Bible Hub, accessed January 9, 2021, https://biblehub.com/greek/1247.htm.

Chapter 5: A Friend Who Brings Us Permanent Peace

1. *NAS New Testament Greek Lexicon*, s.v. "Perispao," Bible Study Tools, accessed January 9, 2021, https://biblestudytools.com/lexicons/greek/nas/perispao .html.

2. Warren Wiersbe, *The Wiersbe Bible Commentary: New Testament*, 2nd ed. (Colorado Springs: David C Cook, 2007), 172.

3. *The Metropolitan Tabernacle Pulpit: Sermons Preached and Revised by C. H. Spurgeon during the Year 1871*, vol. 17 (London: Passmore & Alabaster, 1872), 574.

4. Ralph F. Wilson, "Mary Listens while Martha Labors," JesusWalk Bible Studies, accessed January 10, 2021, http://jesuswalk.com/luke/047-mary-martha.htm.

5. *Helps Word Studies*, s.v. "agathós," Bible Hub, accessed January 10, 2021, https://biblehub.com/greek/18.htm.

6. *Helps Word Studies*, s.v. "eklegó," Bible Hub, accessed January 10, 2021, https://biblehub.com/greek/1586.htm.

7. Wilson, "Mary Listens," http://jesuswalk.com/luke/047-mary-martha.htm.

8. "Sometimes He Calms the Storm," track 4 on Scott Krippayne, *Wild Imagination*, World Records, 2007.

9. *Thayer's Greek Lexicon*, s.v. "akouó," Bible Hub, accessed January 10, 2021, https://biblehub.com/thayers/191.htm.

Chapter 6: The Sweetest Name I Know

1. C. Michael Hawn, "History of Hymns: 'There's within My Heart a Melody,'" Discipleship Ministries, United Methodist Church, June 21, 2013, www.umcdiscipleship.org/resources/history-of-hymns-theres-within -my-heart-a-melody.

2. David Guzik, "Luke 9—The Kingdom of God Is Preached and Displayed," *Enduring Word Bible Commentary*, accessed January 10, 2021, https://enduringword.com/bible-commentary/luke-9/.

3. David Peach, "Ten Famous Christian Martyrs," What Christians Want to Know, accessed January 10, 2021, www.whatchristianswanttoknow.com/10 -famous-christian-martyrs/.

4. *Strong's Concordance*, s.v. "mathétés," Bible Hub, accessed January 10, 2021, https://biblehub.com/greek/3101.htm.

5. Louie Giglio, *I Am Not but I Know I AM: Welcome to the Story of God*, rev. ed. (Colorado Springs: Multnomah Books, 2012), 137.

6. "Zach Williams—Story behind the Song—There Was Jesus," video, YouTube, posted November 6, 2019, www.youtube.com/watch?v=BSXtirKi6E.

About the Author

Wendy is the wife of Scott, mother of Blaire and Griffin, author, speaker, and Bible study teacher. She loves lazy Sundays watching golf with her husband, thrift-store shopping with her daughter, and watching building shows with her son.

Wendy is the author of *Hidden Potential: Revealing What God Can Do through You, Wait and See: Finding Peace in God's Pauses and Plans* and the *Wait and See Participant's Guide: A Six-Session Study on Waiting Well*, as well as the *Yes, No, and Maybe: Living with the God of Immeasurably More* book, study guide, and video series. She is a contributing author to the *Real-Life Women's Devotional Bible, Encouragement for Today: Devotions for Daily Living, The Reason We Speak*, and *God's Purpose for Every Woman*. She leads women all over the world to life change through her in-depth online Bible studies. Down-to-earth and transparent, Wendy teaches in a way that women feel she is speaking directly to their hearts. Her messages are filled with biblical insights and sprinkled with just the right amount of humor to help her audiences see she is a real, everyday woman.

Wendy inspires her audiences to:

- make spending time in God's Word each day a priority
- look for God working around them every day
- view life with a God-first perspective

To bring the message of Jesus Everlasting or another of Wendy's inspiring topics to your next event, contact Wendy at wendy@wendypope.org.

Connect with Wendy

Website: wendypope.org
Email: wendy@wendypope.org
Facebook: www.facebook.com/WendyPopeOfficial
Twitter: @wendybpope
Instagram: WendyPope

About Word Up Ministries

If you were inspired by *Jesus Everlasting* and desire to deepen your own personal relationship with Jesus Christ, I encourage you to connect with me through Word Up Ministries. I have led thousands of women through Read Thru the Word (RTW), a study of the *One Year Chronological Bible*.

Word Up Ministries is a 501(c) (3) nonprofit whose purpose is to nurture and enhance the spiritual growth of Christians all over the world through the teaching of God's Word; to teach those who are not Christians about Jesus and His saving grace, so they might be saved; and to produce and distribute biblical content through video, social media, and written formats in order to disciple and help mature the faith of every member.

We have had the privilege of leading over five thousand men and women through the *One Year Chronological Bible—NLT*. We look forward to broadening the reach of God's Word through Word Up Ministries by continuing our daily teachings and exploring avenues of ministry. To discover more about or support Word Up Ministries, visit www.wordupministries.org.

Bible Credits

Unless otherwise noted, all Scripture quotations are taken from the Holy Bible, New Living Translation, copyright © 1996, 2015 by Tyndale House Foundation. Used by permission of Tyndale House Publishers, Carol Stream, Illinois 60188. All rights reserved.

Scripture quotations marked AMPC are taken from the Amplified® Bible (AMPC), Copyright © 1954, 1987 by The Lockman Foundation. Used by permission. www.Lockman.org.

Scripture quotations marked ESV are taken from the ESV® Bible (The Holy Bible, English Standard Version®), copyright © 2001 by Crossway, a publishing ministry of Good News Publishers. Used by permission. All rights reserved.

Scripture quotations marked EXB are taken from The Expanded Bible, Copyright © 2011 Thomas Nelson Inc. All right reserved.

Scripture quotations marked GW are taken from GOD'S WORD® © 1995, 2020 by God's Word to the Nations Mission Society. Used by permission.

The author has added italics to Scripture quotations for emphasis.

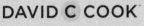

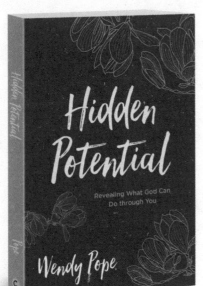